Modern
Whitetail Hunting

Michael Hanback

Published by

 **krause publications**
An F&W Publications Company

700 East State Street • Iola, WI 54990-0001
715-445-2214 • 888-457-2873
www.krause.com

Our toll-free number to place an order or obtain a free catalog is
800-258-0929.

Edited by Joel Marvin
Designed by Wendy Wendt

Library of Congress Catalog Number: 2003108890
ISBN: 0-87349-538-1

Printed in the United States of America

Contents

About the Author. 4
Acknowledgments. 5
Introduction. 7

Chapter 1 The New Breed of Buck. 9
Chapter 2 Scouting for Mr. Big 25
Chapter 3 Buck Triggers. 42
Chapter 4 Taming the Wind 53
Chapter 5 Modern Scent Tricks 62
Chapter 6 Real-World Deer Calling 72
Chapter 7 Rise and Shine 83
Chapter 8 Strike Early. 94
Chapter 9 Super Rut Sets 113
Chapter 10 Pressure Plans 130
Chapter 11 Last-Chance Bucks 141
Chapter 12 Backyard Bucks. 153
Chapter 13 Whitetail Myths & Misconceptions. 165
Chapter 14 Big-Buck Dilemmas 177
Chapter 15 Western Whitetails 188
Chapter 16 Canada's Monster Whitetails 197
Chapter 17 Practical Deer Management. 208

Index 218

About the Author

Virginia's Michael Hanback is one of the foremost hunting writers in the world today. He is a columnist and contributing editor for *American Hunter*, *Outdoor Life* and *Whitetail Hunting Strategies*. Hanback has hunted most species of North American big game over the past 25 years, but his passion remains whitetails. He goes for big bucks with bow and gun in five to 10 states and Canadian provinces each fall. Many of Hanback's hunts appear on Mossy Oak's television shows and videos.

Acknowledgments

I came up with the idea for *Modern Whitetail Hunting* about a decade ago. But before I hit the word processor, I had to hit the road. In my opinion, to write a good, solid book on whitetails, you can't just shoot a few deer around home and use those experiences to build and support your theories. Especially not in this day and age, when whitetail habitat and the behavior of bucks are changing rapidly. You need to get out there to hunt and observe big deer wherever they are found across North America. So I packed my bows and guns and set out to hunt in as many states as I could, and I even visited three Canadian provinces. Man, it was fun!

Over the years and along the way, I met and hunted with some incredible people: David Hale, Harold Knight, Chuck Jones, Will Primos, Jim Crumley, Gary Roberson and Mark and Terry Drury to name just a few. These guys are not only my good friends, but they are also, without question, some of the best deer hunters in the world. Their amazing insight into the ways of the whitetail, and many of the techniques they showed me, are major parts of this book.

As it should be, a writer can never pen a book on deer hunting until he first pays his dues and publishes hundreds or even thousands of magazine articles on the subject. To that end, I owe a special debt of gratitude to: Gerry Bethge of *Whitetail Hunting Strategies*; John Zent of the NRA's *American Hunter*; Todd Smith and Frank Miniter of *Outdoor Life*; and Brian Lovett of Krause Publications. You guys are my favorite editors, and you helped to build my credibility with millions of deer hunters across the country. You also helped pay the bills as I gallivanted around and hunted big bucks.

Finally, I need to thank Toxey Haas, Darrell Daigre, Ronnie "Cuz" Strickland, Troy Ruiz and all the folks at Mossy Oak camouflage for believing in me and throwing their considerable weight and support behind this book. One thing I have learned about the Mossy Oak people is that they are not only hard-core hunters, but also some of the leading conservationists and deer managers in the nation. Working with them to bring you *Modern Whitetail Hunting* was both an honor and a pleasure.

Across the country and especially in the Midwest, hunters are shooting more and more good bucks during the post-rut. I killed this 8-pointer in Iowa in mid-December. Have you been quitting too early each season?

Introduction

A porch light blinked on a mile away ... a dog started barking ... a car door slammed ... a groggy-eyed commuter fired up his SUV ... Years ago I would have shuddered at all that racket. But now, I just sit patiently in my tree stand, paying it no mind, and wait for a buck.

He ghosted through the woodlot at sunrise, his rack brassy in the new light, his hooves popping the frosty leaves, making my heart leap. I drew my bow; an arrow sliced the chilly air. That dog was barking louder than ever and cars were humming out on the county highway as I climbed down and tagged the heavy 8-pointer.

A backwoods adventure? Hardly. But as you probably know, a hunt like the one above is becoming increasingly common these days.

Even with the ups and downs of the economy, new subdivisions, strip malls and industrial parks keep springing up across the country, and especially in the North, East and South. Growth is not confined to the suburbs either. Developers are carving more and more roads, houses and golf courses into rural fields and woodlands, creating quilts of small, broken habitats. The resulting woodlots, thickets, timber strips and small farms provide excellent edge, food and cover for deer, and as a result herds are booming most everywhere.

It boggles my mind to know there are more than 30 million whitetails in North America today. Without question, more Pope & Young and Boone and Crockett bucks roam the woods and plains than ever before.

These are the good ole days for America's 10 million deer hunters, who spend billions each year to foot the bill for both game and non-game management. Hunters' dollars have funded state agencies and played the key role in making the whitetail boom the number one conservation success story in the history of our country.

The opportunity to fill your freezer with venison and put a big rack on the wall has never been better. But to do it, you can't always rely on the hunting tricks your daddy and granddaddy taught you. As their habitat has changed, so too has the behavior and travel patterns of mature bucks. Today, you need innovative tactics, or at least fresh spins on tried-and-true strategies. That is where this book comes in. I packed it with a mother lode of cutting-edge methods that I believe will make you more successful, no matter where you live and regardless of whether you hunt with bow or gun.

As I traveled across North America and researched this book, I found that in two places—the American West and western Canada—the whitetail habitat actually hadn't changed much. There, the country is still big and unspoiled. And the big-buck hunting is also hotter than ever. For a change of pace from hunting a small tract or a pressured public area near home, you might want to head west or north for a crack at a big deer. If so, I've added chapters to help you out.

I wrapped this book with a chapter on managing whitetails on private lands, which is perhaps the hottest trend of all these days. It is without a doubt the wave of the future, and I urge you to get into it now. The big point I want to make is that you don't have to be a large landowner or a millionaire to manage deer. Lease as many acres as you can, and put in a few food strips or plots. Update your thinking to let immature bucks walk. Harvest a good number of does to control your herd and improve its sex ratio. In a short time, you, your buddies and your kids will see healthier bucks with larger racks. Best of all, you'll enjoy awesome hunting for years to come.

Now, on to the modern tactics that will help you see and shoot more big bucks.

Chapter 1

The New Breed of Buck

In some ways, whitetails still exhibit the same traits and behaviors as the deer your daddy and granddaddy hunted. In other ways, they are entirely different cats. For one thing, and this is the good news, many of today's mature bucks are heavier of body and wear larger racks.

Whitetails are everywhere these days! In late summer or early fall, it's not unusual to spot a bachelor's club feeding and mingling in the middle of a subdivision. Come bow season, the biggest buck will live close by. Hunt him if you can.

This is especially true in agricultural regions, like the Midwest, and on large, private grounds where people are planting high-quality food plots and managing the sex ratio and the age structure of deer herds. But it is also the case in some smaller "checkerboard habitats" across the East, North and South. In suburban and once-rural areas, the construction of new houses, roads, golf courses and the like has created a mosaic of clearings, thickets and strips and pockets of woods. Offering plenty of browse and cover, this is perfect habitat for whitetails. The kicker is that by choice or necessity, there is limited hunting in some urban and suburban areas, and that allows bucks to live 3 years or longer and to grow big racks. Within these areas, a good number of 130- to 160-inch bucks can be found.

On the flip side of the coin, there are too many deer—50 or more per square mile—in some fast-developing areas of the North, Mid-Atlantic and South. Here, with so much competition among the whitetails for food, some bucks are stunted and smaller than the deer your ancestors hunted.

One of the themes of this book is that the home ranges and core areas of mature bucks are shrinking across the nation. While years ago a big deer might have routinely roamed 5 miles or more, he might now live his entire life on a 500- to 800-acre farm that offers plenty of quality food year-round, and plenty of does for breeding during the rut. This is more good news for the modern deer hunter. Once you find a big buck on a property, you can often hunt him right there all season. If you don't get him one fall, you might get him the next, and he'll likely have an even larger rack.

What it all means is that to have fun and hunt effectively these days, you need to understand some things about the new breed of buck you're after.

Buck Biology

There are 17 subspecies of white-tailed deer across North America. As a rule, the farther north you go, the heavier the deer. For example, a mature buck of the Northwestern or Dakota subspecies in Alberta or Saskatchewan will stand 40 inches high at the shoulder and strain the scales at 300 pounds or more. Down in Alabama, you might shoot a 2 ½– or 3 ½–year old buck that weighs 130 to 150 pounds on the hoof. He might have short legs and measure only 14 or 15 inches from the bottom of his brisket to his spine.

But as alluded to earlier, the body weights of bucks vary widely these days, depending on the food sources, deer density and genetics in an area.

This 300-pound Saskatchewan bruiser dwarfs the Alabama buck on the right. Both are mature animals with awesome racks.

The bottom line is that you never know what size buck you'll see tip-toeing through the woods, which is quite intriguing.

One word of caution, though—the smaller a buck's body, the larger his 8- or 10-point antlers will appear. I've killed bucks in Alabama and especially in Texas that I swore would score 140 or 150 inches. When I walked up to the diminutive deer, I found their racks to be in the 120 to 130 range. They were still good deer, and I was happy and fortunate to shoot them. Their antlers were just a lot smaller than they first appeared.

Throughout this book you'll read the term "mature buck" many times. I use it to characterize a deer that has lived 3-½ years or longer. These days, if a 3 ½-year-old buck with a nice 8- or 10-point rack walks by the average hunter, especially on public ground, he will and *should* whack him. It should be noted that many biologists, deer managers and trophy hunters don't consider a buck to be mature until he reaches 4-½. The Quality Deer Management Association (QDMA) refers to a 5 ½- or 6 ½-year-old buck as mature or "prime age."

Obviously, you want to shoot the oldest, biggest buck you can. To do that, you must be willing to let yearling and 2 ½-year-old bucks walk and grow. And you must be able to age and field-judge bucks on the hoof at

This is a dream buck in most parts of the country. The 8-pointer is at least 3 ½ years old and his rack scores 140. Note the long tines. That's how a buck really racks up inches of score.

least reasonably well. With the help of the good folks at the QDMA, I put together the following chart to help you out. It will give you a good track to run on, though it certainly won't reflect the body and antler development of every buck in your area. The only way to get really good at field-judging whitetails is to scout and hunt hard, observing and studying lots of bucks of various age classes.

Aging Whitetail Bucks On The Hoof

1.5 years

- Resembles a doe with antlers
- Body appears sleek; no defined muscles
- No swollen neck
- Spike to small 6- or 8-point rack
- Antler spread less than 14 inches

Way too many immature bucks like this get shot each fall. Pass him up and let him grow.

2.5 years

- Thin shoulders and waist
- Distinct junction between neck and shoulders
- Limited neck swelling during the rut
- Maybe nicely developing antlers, but with light mass
- Rack only 60 percent of its potential

3.5 years

- Thickly muscled neck during the rut, but still noticeable junction between neck and shoulders
- Chest appears deeper than hindquarters
- The look of well-conditioned racehorse
- Nice rack—75 percent of its potential
- Typically 8 or more points; inside spread 15 inches or more; main beams 18+ inches; good overall mass

Now this is a shooter. Notice the buck's thick neck and short, blocky face. Oh yeah, what a rack!

4.5 years and older
- Muscular neck blends into shoulders
- Thick, massive appearance; waistline deep as chest
- May have "sway back" and potbelly
- Short, thick face with "squinty eyes"
- Eight- or 10-point rack 80 to 100 percent developed; heavy overall mass; may have "kickers" or other non-typical points

Buck Senses

A buck that lives to the ripe old age of 3-$\frac{1}{2}$ or 4-$\frac{1}{2}$ is nobody's fool. He is an unpredictable, largely nocturnal devil. A big deer relies on his three major senses, which he has adapted nicely to his modern habitat to elude predators, including you and me.

Biologists refer to whitetails as crepuscular animals, meaning they are most active in the twilight. While a buck's vision is geared for low-light conditions, he also sees well on bright, sunny days. The big, cat-marble eyes on the sides of a deer's head provide an exceptionally wide field of view. A buck's monocular vision enables him to pick up a small, fast movement in a flash.

Your old Uncle Joe might have told you that whitetails are colorblind, but modern research has disproved that myth. Scientists have found that deer see some colors, especially blue and yellow tints. But you can easily defend that by wearing a good modern camouflage like Mossy Oak Break-Up. Adding a blaze orange vest or cap during gun season is no big deal. If you sit still and move smoothly at the right time, a buck won't pick you off.

These days, except perhaps for the wilds of Canada, whitetails have grown accustomed to seeing cars and people. The animals have adapted a sort of "ho-hum" attitude, and they seem to sense that human activity on the fringes of their habitat poses no grave threat. But you'd better be careful when you step onto a farm or into the woods and inside a big deer's core area. Unless you take a hidden route to your stand and use brush and trees to help cover your moves, a buck will see you and spook a lot of the time.

It is no old wives' tale that deer look up more than ever these days. Many times on heavily bow-hunted lands in the East and South, I've sat and watched old bucks walk through the woods, scanning the treetops for the lurking silhouettes of hunters. Come to think of it, I'd like to have $100 for every buck that has walked in, peered up at my stand and busted me as I shifted my body or feet to set up the shot, or as I was drawing my bow.

Something I find interesting is that in the Midwest, and especially out West and up into Canada, deer hardly ever look up. You can hang a tree stand 12 to 15 feet high, watch a buck stroll into an open shooting lane 20 or even 10 yards away, and then draw your bow in his face and shoot. My read on it is simple. Where deer are not hunted so heavily from tree stands, they have not adapted to looking up. But if you "sky hunt" in the East or especially down in Alabama or Mississippi, you'd better be still and on your best behavior or you'll get busted.

A deer's ears are 6 to 8 inches long, and they work like tiny satellite dishes, tipping back and forth and rolling around to pick up sounds in all directions. While deer hear extremely well, most impressive to me is how they hone in on a sound—maybe a single grunt or a rattling volley—and know exactly where it came from.

Some scientists now believe that a deer's ears are finely tuned to pick up high-pitched sounds. From my field research, I agree. I believe a buck can hear the clinking of a chain on a tree stand on the hike in, or the clang of a bow or gun against a stand during a hunt, from hundreds of yards away on a calm day. To a buck loafing in his core area, you might as well play heavy metal music. Those unnatural sounds will put him on high alert.

These days, deer have adapted to all sorts of human sounds. How many times have you sat and watched does and bucks feeding in a field as cars popped gravel on a nearby road ... or maybe some guy cranked up a chain saw a half-mile away ... or a dog started barking? Most of the time, the deer never look up from their meal. Again, it's what goes on *inside* a big deer's turf that matters. If a buck hears you bolting home a bullet, or if your treestand pops or squeaks on a calm, crisp morning, he'll jerk up his head and look your way. If he sees movement and puts two and two together, he'll leave the area, either flagging away or, more likely, simply melting off into the brush.

Deer have a tougher time hearing, and picking up movement for that matter, on breezy days. I've read many times that bucks don't move often when it's windy for those very reasons. But that is not always the case, especially out on the plains where the wind blows almost all the time. On many hunts in 10 to 20 mph winds across the country, I've spotted 140- to 160-class bucks prowling around as if it were a bluebird afternoon.

Unless it's blowing a gale, don't let the wind keep you out of the deer woods. Actually, you can use the conditions to your advantage. When the wind rattles the woods and shakes the leaves and grass, you can get away with a little more movement and noise, whether hunting from a tree stand or stalking. A buck simply can't see or hear you as well.

The whitetail's sense of smell is legendary. That is why I devoted Chapter 4 to taming the wind, and Chapter 5 to using scents and actually appealing to a buck's powerful sniffer. But here I'd like to make a couple of points.

First, some scientists believe that whitetails smell best when and where the air is warm and moist. I second that. That is precisely why deer in the deep, humid South can smell you up to a half-mile away. If an old doe winds you in a stand, or if she cuts your lingering scent where you hiked in an hour earlier, she will stop and start stamping her foot and blowing, sometimes for 5 minutes or longer. Hunting from Virginia down through Mississippi, I've watched bucks cut my scent stream, turn inside out and run for the hills. You have to admire the Southern whitetail's incredible sense of smell, though it sure makes the hunting tough.

In my experience, deer in arid, open regions—north Texas, Wyoming or Montana, for example—don't wind you nearly as badly as their Eastern kin. The scenting conditions are not all that great, and to detect danger, open-country deer seem to rely more on their eyesight than their noses. You still have to play smart out West, especially when using a bow, but you can often get away with hunting a big deer on a marginal wind.

Whitetails have also skewed their sense of smell to their modern surroundings. In heavily populated areas, the animals have grown accustomed to smelling car exhaust, joggers and even burgers smoking on grills. But if they smell a rat—in this case you—in a nearby woodlot, the gig is up. Again, it is what a buck sees, hears or smells inside his core area that determines his behavior and movements.

Buck Reflexes

Watch a buck jump a fence or highway, and it is easy to see he's one quick, agile dude. His reflexes are awesome too, and although they don't come into play that much when you carry a gun, it's another matter when you bow hunt.

© Charles J. Alsheimer

A heavyweight buck is an agile critter, able to leap a fence, creek or road in a single bound. His eyes and ears are great, and his nose is awesome. A big deer will bust you and be gone in a flash if you give him half a chance.

You've got to read the body language of every buck that approaches your bow stand. If a big deer is calm and strolling alone with hips swiveling gently as he browses or noses the ground, then you've won half the battle. He is not wired to hear your bow go off where he could try to "duck the arrow." Years ago hunters called it "jumping the string," but that is a misnomer. When a buck (or an old doe for that matter) reacts to the sound of the shot, he typically drops his chest to the ground and wheels back the way he came in one continuous motion. You can't see it with your naked eye, but you can see it and gawk in amazement if you slo-mo a video of a bow hunter shooting at a buck.

A deer that is wired and jittery—maybe he sees or smells something he doesn't like, or maybe he senses a rival buck in the area—is the one most apt to duck an arrow. When that happens, even inside 20 yards, you're apt to hit the buck high above the lungs or shoot over him altogether. The latter is actually preferred over wounding a deer.

You need to work a buck's reflexes into your shooting plan, especially if you bow hunt in the East or South, where deer always seem to be walking on eggs. When a buck is broadside or quartering away, aim at the lower third of his vitals. If he does not react much to the twang of the bow-string, you'll make a perfect low-lung or heart shot. If a deer looks tense or nervous as a cat, you might place a sight pin lower yet—say on the bottom of his chest—though still on hair. Then when he reacts to the shot, he should drop into the plane of your arrow where you have a good chance to double-lung him.

Big Deer Individuality

We writers and talking heads on TV and videos are always telling you how mature bucks go here and there, and do this and that. Big deer do have tendencies, but I believe they are more individualistic than we give them credit for.

Some bucks, like people, are born aggressors, and they become increasingly brazen as they age. They travel widely and lay down lots of big, violent rubs and scrapes. During the rut, they won't back down from a good scrap over a hot doe. Heck, the warmongers often pick fights with rival bucks. These bad boys are the ones you see chasing does full bore across fields and down funnels in the woods.

Some bucks are aggressive and paw like mad. Other deer are more laid back and scrape less. Peak scraping occurs from October 20 through November 4 in Central and Northern states.

I have noticed that other bucks, like other people, are more laid back. When they are young, they probably avoid major confrontations. As they mature, perhaps even to dominant status, they don't go looking for fights. A prime-age, 150- or 160-inch buck with an easygoing manner might even back down from a rival, even though he could easily whip the intruder's butt. An aloof deer figures he doesn't need the hassle, so he wanders off to another core area close by in search of does.

A laid-back deer, which I believe blazes far fewer rubs and scrapes than his rough-and-tumble kin, ambles along and noses out estrous does during the rut, but he might not chase them helter-skelter. He typically corrals a hot gal and carts her off to a secluded thicket, where he does his thing away from the commotion of young and other old bucks.

I believe that anytime you can hunt an aggressive buck, you've got a pretty good shot at scoring big. Scout for his large, plentiful sign and piece it together. Since the deer is energetic and moves a lot, there is a decent chance he'll make a mistake and let you eyeball him in daylight hours. He might stroll into an alfalfa field or oak flat an hour before dark one afternoon early or late in the season, and he might spend some busy time out in the open each morning. When he's rutting, you might see him anywhere and at anytime. If the timing of your rattling is right late in the pre-rut, this type of buck is stoked to respond.

On the other hand, a big, mild-mannered deer is a tougher nut to crack. You may glimpse a 150-incher sneaking through the woods a couple of times, yet be unable to find much big sign in the area, even deep into the pre-rut. That is because the deer probably isn't rubbing or scraping much. He can't help, however, but leave wide, deep 3- to 4-inch tracks on field edges and at river or creek crossings, and that is the sign to look for in these cases.

Chances are a buck like this won't approach a food source until right at dark, or after dark, early in the season, and especially later in the fall once he's been hassled by hunters for a few weeks. And although he probably won't rumble across a pasture or down a funnel after a doe, he will move, feed and breed at his own leisurely pace, which makes your plan simple. To see him, spend a lot of hours in your best stands.

Home Ranges & Core Areas

As I mentioned earlier, and as you will read many more times in this book, the home ranges and core areas of mature bucks are getting smaller and smaller. And it seems the longer a buck lives, the more his territory shrinks. I'm convinced that if a 500-acre farm or ranch has lots of high-quality food and is home to several groups of does, which have even smaller home ranges than the bucks, at least one big deer will live there year-round.

In recent years I've interviewed many experts and hunters from across the country—people who have shot awesome deer scoring from

The home core areas of bucks are shrinking. If a 500-acre farm has lots of crops and plenty of cover, several big shooters will live there year-round.

150 to 200 Boone and Crockett points. Inevitably, these hunters tell me something like, "I saw the buck a few times, and he was always in the same general area." Not long ago a friend of mine shot a 210-inch buck (gross score), with a bow I might add, on his 400-acre Iowa farm. He told me he spotted the deer several times in food plots and crop fields during the summer and early fall. He shot him 200 yards away in the woods when the rut got kicking in November.

Some bucks, especially those hard-charging ones we talked about, have larger home ranges than others. Within any home range, be it 500 to 1000 acres, are small "core areas" where big deer spend most of their time, especially during the rut-preparation phase of late summer and early fall. A mature buck might expand his range in search of does when the rut comes, but he'll usually return home once the breeding season is over. So for obvious reasons, you need to find the best core areas. Here are the key ingredients to look for.

The more feed on a property, the more time a buck will spend there. It's just that simple. If a farm or ranch has a couple of soybean, corn or alfalfa fields—or better yet a mix of crops—that's great. But one or even two major food sources aren't really enough. Suppose there's a drought one year. What if in early fall a farmer picks clean his grain? Well, according to many biologists, a buck has to eat not just once, but several times each day. If forced, he'll quickly expand his range in search of quality feed.

Ideally, a tract will have crops, food plots *and* a variety of other food sources to sustain deer throughout autumn and early winter, the times when you are out there with bow or gun. Look in the woods for a blend of oaks, the lifeline of the whitetail in many regions. White oak acorns mature annually, while red oaks make nuts every couple of years. That's how nature puts some mast on the ground every fall.

Crops and acorns are the anchors that keep bucks home on most lands. But down South deer eat pecans. Up North they crunch beechnuts. Whitetails anywhere love persimmons, honey locust pods, crabapples, wild cherries and other soft mast. Browse like sumac, dogwood and honeysuckle are staples, especially late in the season. Look for secondary stuff like that.

If you hit paydirt and find a smorgasbord, you know the soils on a property are good. Minerals from the earth and the nutritious foods will help some of the resident bucks grow heavy racks.

Three tiers of food sources are perfect whitetail habitat.

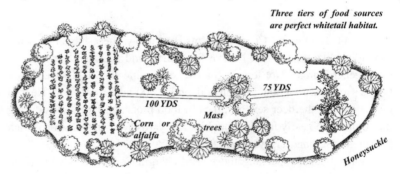

Figure 1. *The more food sources on your hunting land the better.*

For a deer to live at least 3-½ years and grow big headgear, he needs cover and lots of it. Some biologists say the ideal habitat is comprised of 30 percent brush and edge.

When evaluating a property, check for thinned or cutover woods, regenerating burns, overgrown fields, CRP strips … you get the picture. Deer are fringe animals. They love to travel edges, lingering here and there to browse greenery and snack on the soft mast that often grows there.

Look for does to bed in the big covers. Then expect mature bucks to hole up in "satellite thickets" nearby. Small cattail swamps, cedar patches, tangled fencerows and especially ridge thickets are great places to start. The more satellites you find near spots where does feed and bed, the better. When the rut and hunting pressure heat up, old bucks cruise from cover to cover, utilizing several core-bedding areas.

To my mind, a big-buck hotspot beyond compare is laced with creeks, sloughs or maybe a river. Deer drink of the free water, especially in a hot, dry fall and when chasing during the rut. But moreover, a water source with rich soils, diverse plant life and brushy edges provides deer with the key elements of food and cover. Studies show that wherever possible, whitetails gravitate to and reside in fertile drainages. Remember that when checking out potential places to lease and hunt.

© Charles J. Alsheimer

When looking for land to lease, hone in on a property with creeks, sloughs or a river. The rich soils and diverse plant life around water provide whitetails with the key elements of food and cover.

A couple more things help to make a big-buck area complete. The more old roads and rights-of-way that cut a property, the better. I've found that across the country, bucks love to rub and scrape in brushy logging roads. Both does and bucks browse, bed and travel in power-line or gas-line cuts, but you've got to limit foot travel and ATVs in these areas for the hunting to be good.

Also, check for draws, ravines, ridge saddles, strips of timber between fields, brushy fencerows, necked-down creek crossings and the like. One constant with the new breed of bucks is that, regardless of where they live in North America, they use funnels when trading back and forth between feeding and bedding grounds. Big deer troll for and chase does in those funnels when the rut kicks in. Remember that and work it into your plan, whether you hunt a 20-acre woodlot, a 500-acre farm or a sprawling national forest.

Whether you hunt a 20-acre woodlot or a 1000-acre property, key on brushy draws, finger ridges and similar funnels that link feeding and bedding areas. That's where you see and shoot bucks.

Chapter 2

Scouting for Mr. Big

Before you can hunt a big deer, you must find him. Sounds elementary, but think about it. A buck that lives 3 or 4 years or longer is a survivor. How do you think he keeps growing that gnarly rack of bone on his head? It's not by standing around and waiting for you or me to stumble across him.

Only a buck with a muscular neck and a heavy rack can maul a cedar like this. The bigger the rubs the better!

In a modern, checkerboard habitat with plenty of feed, a mature buck typically prowls a home range of only 400 to 600 acres. A master of deception, he slips around mostly at night and in cover. During daylight hours, he pulls vanishing acts that would make Copperfield proud. Besides filling his gut several times a day and breeding as many does as he can for a few weeks in the fall, Mr. Big's mission is to elude predators, including you and me.

See what I mean? You can't just sit back and wait for an old buck to come to you. You need to take the game to him. Get out there and scout—a lot. Start by narrowing your hunting country, be it public or private land, and looking for the core areas where a big deer hangs out. Then begin to link together his sign. Scouting is not rocket science, but it does require time, effort and a solid plan.

Take A Hike

One day in June or July, when other guys are bass fishing or golfing, lather on the bug dope, lace up your boots and hike every inch of your hunting areas. It will give you a leg up on your competition when the season opens in a few months.

Walk the fence lines and other perimeters of a property first, and gradually work your way into the inner terrains. In the muggy, green woods you're not so much looking for deer sign as trying to get a handle on how the land lays. Carry and consult aerial and topographical maps as you hike draws, ridges, creek bottoms and other terrain where you might someday encounter mature bucks.

Think thick. A 2-acre brier tangle, a field over-grown with grass and cedars, a regenerating cutover, a swath of sec-ond-growth timber ... you get the picture. Wherever you're pushing and sweating your way through a tough patch

Think thick and small. A 2-acre brier patch near a field or a strip of brush on a ridge is all it takes to hide a monster buck.

one summer day, figure that is where a good buck might hide out come fall, especially once the guns start booming in November or December. So what if you spook some deer, including Mr. Big, now? The animals will forget all about your summer intrusion by the time hunting season rolls around.

Check for thickets on hillsides, ridges and bluffs. Mark those spots with big "Xs" on your maps. Old bucks love to bed high and with their backs to the wind, where they smell the rising thermals and scan the woods below for other deer as well as predators.

Investigate river bottoms and creek drainages with that established mix of food, water and cover. Years ago, a biologist told me, "Don't you know that whitetails are creek bottom animals? Find water and you'll find deer." Man, was that guy right. Whether I scout new ground near home in Virginia or out in Missouri or Montana, I check my maps for a creek or river bottom and start my scouting right there.

You need to keep in mind that does and fawns live in the best habitats in any given area. Bucks make out quite nicely in the rough-hewn fringes. Three, four or more groups of does might inhabit a long, linear creek or river drainage with a good blend of food and cover. Find where the does live early on. It lays the groundwork for hunting the rut, when bucks will come calling.

Find the Food

As you will read several times in this book, outside the peak of the rut, most of your strategies should revolve around the food sources of whitetails. When you're out scouting in the summer, pay close attention to any corn, alfalfa or soybean fields planted on your hunting land, as well as on bordering farms. But don't stop there. Go a step further and find out when the crops will be harvested.

One July day in Virginia, I stopped and knocked on a farmer's door. The old-timer eyed me suspiciously, until I told him I didn't want permission to hunt his land. "I hunt the Johnson woods next door," I said. "Your corn looks great. I was just wondering when you plan to cut it?"

I guess I looked harmless enough because the man loosened up and drawled, "Well, I reckon around the second week of September. Tell old Johnson I said hello, and good luck to you."

I thanked the man and left with some vital MRI—most recent information. Come the October archery season, I figured does and bucks

© Charles J. Alsheimer

Anywhere in the country, the planting and harvesting of grain fields has a huge impact on whitetail movement. As feed fields change in an area from year to year, so too does the bed-to-feed patterns of bucks.

would feed and mingle in the farmer's cut corn at night. I reckoned some of the deer would then filter back to bed in the woods and thickets where I hunted a mile away. Well, I figured right. One morning I climbed into a stand on a ridge and arrowed a heavy 10-pointer returning from the field to hide out for the day.

Suppose, however, the farmer had told me that he wouldn't pick his corn until late October or even November? Well, the local does and bucks might have exhibited a polar opposite pattern. A lot of deer might have bedded throughout the early season in the standing corn. Every couple of days, some animals might have made rounds into my woods to feed on acorns or soft mast. I might have had to flip-flip my routine and hunt more from evening stands positioned downwind of feeding areas.

Anywhere in the country, the planting and harvesting of corn, alfalfa, soybeans or other crops have a big—no, make that huge—influence on the bed-to-feed patterns of whitetails. Monitor the grain fields in and around your hunt zones, get that MRI and tailor your morning and afternoon setups accordingly.

When acorns ripen and fall in September or October, does and bucks will come from near and far to fatten up for the rut.

On a summer hike, carry a binocular and glass the treetops for green mast, especially white or red oak acorns. When nuts and soft fruits ripen and begin falling in September or October, does and bucks will come from near and far to fatten up for the rut. Somewhere near productive mast trees is where you need to hunt when the early archery season opens.

Seeing is Believing

On soft and sultry evenings in July, August and early September, many old bucks feed and posture their racks for does and subdominant males in fields of clover, soybeans, alfalfa and the like. No fields in your hunt zone? No problem. A good buck or two or maybe even a "bachelor's club" might strut their stuff in a low-grass burn, clear-cut or gas right-of-way carved out in the woods.

Drive to a spot, hide your truck and sneak up a hill 400 yards or so off a field or woodland opening. With a quality 8X or 10X binocular and a 15X to 45X spotting scope, glass for mature bucks at dusk. The color of mocha and rimmed in velvet, their antlers will look a third again bigger than when they're hard and polished a month or so later. Still, you'll have no trouble zeroing in on one or two awesome racks to hunt.

Now, forget about that rack. Glass *beyond* Mr. Big and study the woods and thickets where he stepped out. Look for a fencerow, ditch, timber strip or similar funnel that spills out into the field or woodland opening. Where and how far does that funnel run back into the cover? Think back to your earlier scouting hikes and consult your aerial or topo map for the answers. Begin to put things together.

Four fresh tracks with a giant buck standing in them are the best sign of all. You cannot glass too much! Once you spot a big deer, he'll live close. Move in and hunt him when the wind and conditions are right.

Say, for example, a whopper 8-pointer pops out into an alfalfa field in roughly the same spot three evenings in a row. Studying an aerial photo, you figure the deer is sneaking off a ridge a half-mile away and dropping down into a creek bottom before veering off into the field. Voila! You've narrowed the country and found a vital link in that buck's bed-to-feed pattern.

Where Did He Go?

Poof! Come mid-September and into early October, especially in the eastern U.S., many bucks vanish from crop fields where they fed and postured weeks earlier. The main reason is that acorns and other mast start dropping in the woods, and the deer gorge themselves to fatten up.

Ah, but I believe something else is going on here. Feeling the first tickle of testosterone in the early pre-rut, mature bucks become less gregarious. Many of the big boys get testy, split from bachelor groups and hole up in core areas back in the timber, where they start putting on their game faces for the breeding season.

Once Mr. Big disappears in September or October, who knows where he'll be come hunting season, right? Wrong. I say he'll probably be hanging out within a mile of the field or opening where you spotted him over the summer. He's just not very visible.

© Charles J. Alsheimer

Early in the fall, bucks lie up in thickets near crop fields or oak flats. When the rut erupts, you never know where they'll bed. A big boy might hole up in a copse of brush out in the open, where he can keep an eye on does and other bucks.

Think about it. If you hunt a diverse, broken habitat—say a 200-acre woodlot rimmed with fields and interspersed with thickets and a river or creek—what more would a buck want? He cruises nightly to food sources near his core bedding areas. Come the rut, he trolls for does in nearby draws and drainages. Here's that "homebody theory" of mine again. Once you find a big deer, you can often hunt him *right there* all season.

Crunch Time

Funny, we've come this far without really looking for deer trails, tracks, rubs or scrapes. That's according to plan, because you've got to lay the groundwork. But sooner or later you must go into an area and snoop for the sign that links Mr. Big's movements to your until-now abstract theories. I advise hitting the woods a week or so before archery season in September or October.

Many hunters, including some well-known whitetail authorities, disagree with this strategy. They strongly disagree, howling that you'll make a little noise, stink up the joint and turn a mature buck even more nocturnal than he already is before you ever hunt him. Their philosophy is to stay out of Mr. Big's living quarters until later in the fall, when a rutting buck will move harder and farther in daylight hours and, hence, be easier to hunt.

Those "low impact" guys make some good points. Still, I'll take my chances. Nowadays, you have to figure that you weren't the only hunter who scouted and observed a big deer during the summer months. If you don't go in and go for the buck ASAP, somebody else gladly will, either in your hunt zone or on a bordering property. Another hunter might kill "your" buck, or at least pressure him to the point where you might never see him again.

Also, consider this. You can glass, read maps and speculate all you want about a big deer's movement pattern. But without doing a little ground scouting, how can you predict with reasonable certainty where a buck is feeding, bedding and traveling right now?

You can't, so go for it.

Try to scout on a quiet, rainy day. Go from 10 A.M. until early afternoon, when most deer are bedded back in thickets or woods. Sneak to a field or

Low-impact glassing lays the groundwork for success, but at some point you need to move in and "speed scout" a ridge or bottom. Find a huge rub and you've found a corner of a good buck's core area.

woodland opening where you glassed Mr. Big a few times. Test the wind. It should blow out of the cover, or at least parallel to it.

Follow a deer trail back into the woods and thickets. Use your head and don't walk on or across the trail; stay well off to one side of it. Look for fresh, shiny rubs. Scout for large buck tracks in trails, and in muddy creek crossings. Check to see if oak trees are raining their acorns. If so, you're apt to find a flurry of rubs and "pawings," or early scrapes. Make a couple of quick sweeps through the area, looking for good trees for stands. Then get the heck out of there!

You'll crack a few twigs and rustle some leaves. You'll leave trace scent on the ground and brush. You might even jump a few deer and see them flag away. But so what? These days, whitetails are accustomed to farmers, woodcutters, hikers, squirrel hunters, joggers—all sorts of people roaming back roads and woodlands. A big deer is sharp, but c'mon! Even if a buck sees or smells you, he can't reason that you're coming to hunt him in a few days.

You obviously don't want to spook Mr. Big, but if you do, don't worry about it. The deer won't blow out the woods and run into the next county. He'll head for a thicket somewhere inside his home core area. In a day or two, the buck will settle down and go back to his normal routine. Since you've found his most recent sign, you have a darn good idea of where to hunt him.

In-Season Scouting

Acorns and soft mast drop at various intervals from September through December. Crops are cut as early as September, or picked as late as November. Hunting pressure heats up. Unless a buck is off chasing a doe during the peak of the rut, he'll keep on living where he feels most comfortable—in those thickets and funnels you scouted way back in the summer. But it doesn't take an old survivor long to become wary and nocturnal, and to alter his travel pattern.

That is why you should be on the lookout for new clues every day you hunt. Don't just hike into or out of a stand or blind with your head down and your mind wandering. To the contrary, stay focused and look around for fresh rubs and scrapes. Veer over to check a nearby draw, creek crossing or strip of timber for fresh sets of large tracks. Monitor mast trees, forever looking for ripening nuts and fruits. In a word, scout as much as you hunt to keep tabs on Mr. Big.

Look for fresh tracks and other sign on the hike to and from a stand each day.

On the walk into a tree stand one November afternoon, I angled over for a peek at a gleaming rub that had popped up overnight in a honeysuckle thicket. Man, I found the mother lode—more rubs and fresh scrapes. I wondered, "Should I continue on to my stand a quarter-mile away, or should I take a chance and wing it from the ground right here?" What the heck, I climbed a nearby ridge, plopped down beside a tree and waited.

Thirty minutes before dark, leaves popped and a twig cracked. I eyed the buck through my riflescope. It was the same 8-pointer I'd spotted in August in a clover field a mile away! The same buck that had given me the slip all bow season! I settled the crosshair on Mr. Big. My 270 cracked and 4 months of scouting came full circle.

Look Around

A mature buck is a homeboy. The older he gets, the more his home range and core areas shrink. But there is no denying that a big deer will wander on occasion, especially when he's cruising for does or trying to avoid other bucks during the rut. Heck, the largest segment of a big deer's home range might be across a fence and on land that is off-limits to you.

With that in mind, drive the perimeters of hunting areas a few times each fall. You might not be able to hunt over there, but it never hurts to look. Note draws, creek bottoms, fencerows, strips of trees and the like that run off adjoining properties and onto your turf. Funnels that lead to and from nearby crop fields should really catch your eye.

Big-Buck Sign

- **RUBS** 4 inches or more in diameter are often called "signposts," and mature deer likely blazed them. But because small bucks do occasionally "horn" thick trees, it's sometimes more telling to study the damage done. An old buck has the neck power and rack size to thrash a large hardwood tree, or even snap a pine or cedar. An immature buck with a spindly 6- or 8-point rack can't do that. More big-buck clues: Look for deep tine grooves and gashes high above the heart of a rub, and on branches and trees behind and around it. Look for a rub line that wends out from a signpost and connects a buck's feeding and bedding area. Rub lines can be tough to find and decipher when the foliage is thick in early fall.

You find a big track. Mature doe or buck? Work the puzzle. If you find big rubs and maybe scrapes nearby, you're likely hot on the trail of Mr. Big.

- **TRACKS** that are noticeably long, wide and deep were probably left by a mature buck. Check 3- to 4-inch prints closely. An old buck sometimes has split, cracked or curved hooves; his tracks are distinctive.
- **SCRAPES** can definitely have you chasing your tail. Just remember this: A bunch of rather ordinary-looking scrapes on a field edge or ridge or in a creek bottom were probably pawed by a rather ordinary buck. I've found, and some biologists and whitetail experts second my opinion, that *mature bucks build large scrapes, but fewer of them.* The best way to tell if a big buck dug a scrape is to look around and inside it. Big rubs near a scrape and a huge hoof print inside are the telltale sign of Mr. Big. Any scrape worth a second look will have a mangled "lick branch" overhead.

- **BEDS** are oblong ovals in leaves, matted grass or snow. A single, huge bed in a thicket on a ridge or bluff is sure-fire buck sign. Look for big tracks, droppings and especially monster rubs nearby. Since a buck bedded there at least once, chances are he'll be back. He might not use the same bed, but he'll curl up somewhere on the ridge or bluff.

Any scrape worth a second look will have a mangled "lick branch" overhead.

- **TRAILS** that wend from thickets to fields and course through draws, drainages and other funnels are definitely worth investigating. Major doe paths change as food sources ripen and dry up, and as hunting pressure builds in an area. Still, trails link the major feeding, bedding and breeding zones of whitetails, and you need to monitor them all season. Bucks prowl along and across doe paths throughout the fall and especially during the rut.
- **DROPPINGS** are easiest to find around feeding and bedding areas. Biologists say that a deer defecates about 24 times a day, so if you find a bunch of scat beneath an oak tree or in a secluded swamp, a bunch of deer are spending time there. An old saw says that the bigger the pellets the bigger the doe or buck that dropped them, though some biologists now dispute that. Just work the puzzle. In a spot littered with fresh rubs and large tracks, a buck likely dropped a large clump of scat.

When it comes time to bow or gun hunt, scout the heads of those funnels on your side of the fence. If you find smoking-hot sign, set up and watch for a good buck coming or going.

Key on Change

It never hurts to look! Glass for bucks on neighboring lands. Some of those deer will hop the fence to feed or rut where you can hunt them.

One September day I trucked out to a woodlot where I'd shot several good bucks over the years. I knew the ridges, flats and creek bottoms like the rooms of my house, so I planned only a cursory scout. When the white oak acorns started dropping later in the month, deer would come from miles around, and I pretty much had them patterned.

I hiked past all the familiar landmarks in the woods, but then I spotted something strange, a glinting through the trees. I raised my binocular—aluminum siding ... part of a roof ... a house! They sure build 'em fast these days. A small subdivision had sprung up on the adjacent property over the spring and summer.

Whitetails are adaptable critters, amazingly so. But I figured those new homes, complete with hollering kids and barking dogs, would change the travel routes of the local does and bucks. So to heck with a quick check. I hustled back to my truck, dug a topo map from behind the seat and flew into some serious scouting on my side of the fence.

I walked the property boundaries near the new houses. Sure enough, things had changed. The ridges and hollows that were always littered with deer trails, tracks and rubs were barren.

I pressed on, looking for a draw, finger ridge or linear thicket that might funnel deer off the newly developed ground. Soon I hit paydirt. A little creek drainage wended between two of the 20-acre lots and snaked into a white oak flat on the northwest corner of my turf. Looking closer, I found a narrow crossing pocked with fresh tracks. I hung a stand there in October and arrowed a heavy 8-pointer coming in a roundabout way to the mast on my side of the fence.

These days, houses, roads, golf courses and the like are popping up all over the place. Timber brings premium dollars, so there's a lot of thinning and clear-cutting going on. The activity might not drive deer out of their haunts, but it definitely impacts their travel patterns. As you scout your hunting areas, be certain to monitor developments on adjacent and nearby properties. Again, get that MRI. Mark land changes on your maps and study them. Then scout more and revamp your strategies to coincide with the new deer patterns.

Monitor Pressure

Did you sit in a stand on opening day of gun season last November and hear what sounded like World War II on the next farm? If so, ask around and find out if the same guys will be hunting that property this fall. Probably so, but there's a chance the land was posted over the summer. Either way, you need to know because surrounding pressure, or lack thereof, will dictate deer routes into and out of your hunt zone.

If you determine an army of hunters will fire up 4-wheelers and fire guns on their side of the line, you can begin to formulate a couple of strategies. First, think about watching a cover-laced funnel on your side of the fence during opening week—that mini-riot on the other side might drive a good buck your way. Later in gun season, when bucks become reclusive and highly nocturnal, move deeper into your area. Deer may come from all around to hole up in lightly pressured thickets on your side of the fence.

On the other hand, if you find out that a neighboring property will be tightly posted, great. You can hang tree stands or set ground blinds several hundred yards off the sanctuary on your side of the line, and "rotate hunt" them throughout the season. Even moderate pressure anywhere on the other sides of your area might push a buck toward the posted ground and into your sights.

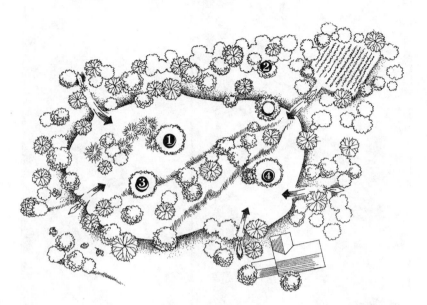

Figure 2. *Stand positions 1 and 3 could be hot if people hunt lands to the west and north of your property. They might inadvertently drive you a buck. Catch a big deer at Stand 2 as he leaves a farmer's cut corn. Stand 4 could be a good spot to bust a buck skirting a new house in the area.*

Scouting Tools

- **Aerial photos:** You simply cannot scout or hunt effectively without black-and-white or color photos of your area. Check with your local extension agency, or check the phone book under "Photographs – Aerial." Some gun and archery shops sell aerial maps as well as topo maps.
- **Clothes:** On a summer hike, spray your Mossy Oak clothes with bug dope. No Stinking Ticks from Scent Shield works great. Juice your clothes with an odor-neutralizer when poking around the woods in early fall.

After every scouting mission, jot down where you spotted bucks and where you found big rubs, trails and scrapes. Review your notes from time to time. Pretty soon deer patterns in the area will begin to develop.

- **Boots:** Wear calf-high rubber "burleys" or modern leather boots lined with a charcoal-activated, scent-blocking material. Tuck pants legs into boots to keep the ticks and chiggers out.
- **Clippers:** Carry a hand clipper to prune briers and vines as you blaze a trail through a thicket in the summer. You'll need clippers and a folding saw to cut out spots for tree stands.

Quick Tip: The mornings and evenings immediately after a farmer cuts a cornfield are good times to scout. The sudden change in the habitat forces deer to alter their bed-to-feed patterns, so they'll move more than usual. Hang back off a freshly cut field and glass for bucks moving around and trying to sort out their new digs.

- **Compass:** You probably won't get lost or turned around on a scouting mission, but use a compass to determine wind direction, sun angles, etc. when considering trees for your stands.
- **Trail cameras:** Shell out a few hundred bucks for a couple of trail cameras and hook them on trees near main trails that empty into fields, mast flats and other major feeding areas. When you capture a photo of a good buck, it not only helps you pattern his movements, it also lights your fire to hunt a particular area.

Chapter 3

Buck Triggers

Some days you spot a bunch of deer, including some thick, gnarly-racked bucks, moving hard in and around fields, woods and funnels. Other days you sit a stand for hours and see a couple of does and fawns, or maybe no animals at all. What gives? What makes the movements of whitetails so darn unpredictable?

© Charles J. Alsheimer

What makes a big deer walk? Outside the peak of the rut, food is the overriding factor.

No scientist or deer-hunting authority worth his salt will claim to have all the answers. I certainly don't. But after many years of observing and hunting whitetails across the United States and Canada, I have gained perspective on five things that impact the natural travel patterns of the game. I call them "buck triggers," and you ought to work them into your game plan.

Food

As mentioned in the previous chapter, most of your strategies should revolve around the many varieties of crops, mast and browse that deer eat. This is especially true early and late in the season. And it never hurts to work food into your rut-hunting plan. Does may look dainty, but they eat like pigs right up until the day they come into estrus. As they move to and from a field or mast flat, they pull glassy-eyed bucks out of hiding.

Say it's late September or early October, and you have permission to bowhunt a field of alfalfa or corn. It's a given that one or two mature bucks will come there not only to fatten up, but also to showboat for does and interact with subdominant bucks. If a field is lightly pressured, you might spot a P&Y deer or several good bucks running in a bache-

Some biologists say whitetails must feed at least a little bit every 4 to 6 hours. The more time you spend in a stand near crops or acorns, the better your chances of tagging a good buck.

lor's club, tipping down a doe trail and into the grain an hour before sundown each day. When whitetails are locked into a bed-to-feed pattern early in the season, the hunting can be that good and predictable.

Evening is the best time to score around a feeding area anytime of the season, but it is not the only time. Research projects have shown that whitetails must feed every 4 to 6 hours to replace food in their rumen. Biologists point out that factors like hunting pressure, hot weather and harsh sunlight suppress some daytime feedings. Still, and I have seen this all over North America, many bucks get up and nibble, if only briefly, a few times each day. So the more time you spend in a stand or blind near crops, acorns or green browse, the better your odds of spotting a big deer *anytime*.

Sometimes an oddball food source will cause deer to move in unusual places, especially late in the season. Out in Iowa one December, I hunted a farm that had it all—large fields and small plots of corn, soybeans, clover and peas. Hmm, strange. Why was I spotting so many does and bucks, including a giant 8-pointer, moving out in nearby CRP fields each evening? Come to find out that earlier in the fall, the farmer had cut and baled strips of the tall, brown grass. I investigated and found that a smorgasbord of tiny, green, broad-leafed weeds had sprouted up in the

Sometimes an oddball food source, like tiny green forbs sprouting up after a farmer's haying or a fall rain, will cause deer to move in unusual places. Keep an eye out for such food sources.

mowed strips. Then I got it. Some deer were ignoring the crops and plots and moving to the succulent, protein-rich forbs. I didn't get the big 8 I was hunting, but I did shoot another good buck following does to the herbs. The point: To see deer, monitor the feed, both the primary and secondary stuff.

Cover

Mature bucks love to bed close to food sources. They seem to sense that the less ground they cover, the better their chances of eluding predators, including you and me. Find a thicket of wild rose, honeysuckle or pines on a ridge within 200 to 400 yards of a crop, food plot field or freshly falling acorns, and I'll bet you $100 that a good buck beds there, at least some days. And there's a good chance that ridge cover is a "hub." A buck's daily travels might start out and end up right there, especially early in the season before the does come into estrus.

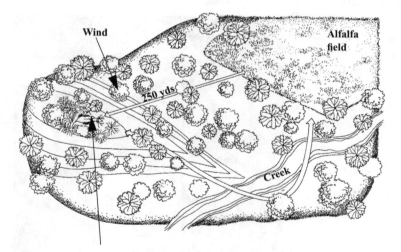

Figure 3. Look for big bucks bedding in ridge thickets near food sources.

I find that like you and me, whitetails like to walk the shortest route between Points A and B. But unless he is drunk on testosterone and goofy for does, rarely will a big deer stroll across a bald field or cutover, or through 200 yards of mature, open timber. Rather, he'll circle several hundred yards and sneak down a ditch, along a brushy edge—you get the idea—to get to where he's going. Look for the big tracks, rubs and scrapes that fringe-hugging bucks leave in their wake.

Weather

Blame it on global warming, El Niño, or whatever. The fact is, we've had a string of unseasonably warm autumns and winters in many regions, and many meteorologists expect the trend to continue well into the future. Since warm weather impacts deer movements in many areas, especially in the Midwest and North, you'd better be ready with some heat-beater tactics.

Let's say it is early in season and before the rut *or* late in the winter and after the major breeding window has closed. One day the wind swings around out of the south or east, and the temperature soars into the 60s or even the 70s. In my experience, some deer will walk in the mornings, but the majority of animals, having moved during the cooler night hours, will lie up in shady cover.

At dusk a good number of does will get up and move toward food sources. Some bucks will climb out of bed and follow the gals. Play

Nothing shuts down deer movement like an autumnal heat wave. Try to get your buck during the first or last cool hour of the day.

the wind and set up close to a crop field or mast flat, or in a nearby travel funnel, and try to whack a buck during the last 30 minutes of shooting light.

On a rainy, humid, 70-degree morning in Mississippi, I shot this 10-pointer skulking back to a swamp 30 minutes after sunrise. The deer probably wouldn't have moved again till dusk or after dark.

I find that when a warm spell overlaps the rut, whitetails chase and breed a lot at night. When their fun is over, does and bucks break hard and fast for cover at dawn. To cut them off, try hanging a tree stand in a satellite thicket 100 yards or so off a swamp, overgrown field or other bedding area. Play the southerly or easterly wind, and set up in cover where trails, tracks, rubs and scrapes are freshest.

Deer lay low throughout a hot and humid day, often bedding on ridges or bluffs above shady creeks with a light, rising breeze. By late afternoon the animals quiver with pent-up energy. When sunlight fades and the air chills just before dark, does and horny bucks jump up and beat hooves for the nearest field, oak flat or other food source.

Does and immature bucks might roll out into a field or flat and begin pigging out. But 3 ½-year-old and grayer bucks, especially if they have been pressured much, typically move hard to thickets 100 yards or so off a feeding site, then stop and stage before ghosting in to scent-check and chase does after dark. Do a speed scout of your area, checking for fresh doe trails and buck sign in staging thickets. Try to figure out the tricky warm winds and evening thermals, and hang a tree stand. You might get lucky at last light.

Every day during deer season, you ought to keep a close eye on the Weather Channel, or log onto www.weather.com. I like the website because you can hone in on your hunting area, and get hourly updates on the wind, precipitation and temperature.

While you can beat the heat and kill big deer, you can never go wrong by hunting on cool days. I find that as a general rule across the country, deer move best on calm, high-pressure days with highs in the 30s or 40s, and lows in the 20s. But that is highly variable, depending on such things as the availability of food and the stage of the rut in an area.

I always watch the Weather Channel for major fronts coming out of the West. As far as deer movement is concerned, some fronts are bad and others are good. Meteorologists point out that a Pacific front that pushes eastward from California brings warm, modified air to many parts of the country. A front like that can shut down deer, in my experience.

What you want to see on your TV or computer, and plan your hunts around, are major fronts and clippers dipping down into the U.S. from northwestern Canada. After a warm spell, cool weather on the backside of a front almost always kicks does and bucks into high gear, or at least into second gear. You'll often have to deal with gusty winds and maybe lingering rain or snow on the backside of a front, but that is when you need to be out there because the bucks should move.

Does

Years ago, big deer had to travel far and wide to scent-check scattered pockets of does. Today, with whitetail populations busting at the seams in most regions, bucks can tool around and visit four or five doe units within a short walk of their core areas. No wonder the home ranges of mature bucks have shrunk dramatically in many areas.

Still, the *location* of does dictates buck movement. Several scientists have told me that anywhere in North America, whitetails are creek bottom animals, and I believe them. A drainage with abundant food and

My theory is that with so many doe units living in close proximity these days, bucks don't have to travel far to have their fun during the breeding season.

cover will hold at least one doe unit. A long, winding river or creek bottom is apt to house three or more groups of does and fawns. Those liner covers are prime places to spot rutting bucks in November, or in December or January in the Deep South.

Moon

There are more moon theories than protein shakes on the market these days. Let me add mine to the mix.

Some American Indians called the 11th full moon of the year the "hunter's moon." Some whitetail authorities now refer to it as the "rutting moon," and they believe it triggers the peak of the whitetail rut in central and northern states and Canadian provinces. Other scientists say hogwash, that deer north of the 36th parallel will breed sometime between November 7 and 20, regardless of when the full moon occurs. Well, I'll leave the bickering to the academics. From a hunter's perspective, my read on it is pretty simple. First, in any given year, the week *before* the rutting moon is a great time to hunt. Moreover, when that

The one lunar theory I have the most confidence in is the oldest one in the book. Many bucks seek, chase and breed does from 9:00 A.M. till 2:00 P.M. during a full moon in early to mid-November. If you're not out there at midday, you're messing up!

week falls in late October or early November, I expect dynamite action, especially when days and nights are seasonably cool.

My friend Mark Drury, who hunts and films trophy bucks across the Midwest, concurs. "We often find the hunting is best when a first-quarter moon exposes the whitetail's seeking phase in late October or early November," he says. "A lot of big deer will go on the prowl."

On morning hunts during a first-quarter moon, hang your tree stand near a line of fresh scrapes, or downwind of a doe-bedding thicket. As bucks troll for the first hot does, it's a fine time to rattle or grunt call. "The hunting should also be good around food sources in the afternoon," adds Drury.

Don't try to find me anytime the moon waxes full in early to mid-November. Every morning I'll be perched in a stand in a cover-laced funnel in the Virginia woods. I might not have much action early—bucks that trolled for does all night in the glowing woods usually bed for a few hours at first light. But around 10:00 or 11:00 on one of those mornings, I *expect* to see a big deer back on his hooves and lollygagging through the timber, nose to the ground and sniffing for a gal. Man, I've smoked some good bucks at midday when a big moon hangs over my state's early muzzleloader season.

I believe the biologists who say that from November 7th to 20th, depending on region, bucks will have a ball, chasing, tending and breeding does. The peak of the rut is obviously a good time to be in the woods. A third-quarter and/or a new moon during this time will really help you out. During the 3 weeks of mostly dark nights, mature bucks should move hard and fast at dawn and dusk. Set up in a timbered or brushy funnel and try to ambush one.

The deeper you hunt into November or early December, the tougher the sledding. From Virginia to Missouri and all points north, nearly all the mature does will have been bred. Also, gun hunters will have spooked and shot a bunch of bucks. The pressure will pretty much shut down the last flurries of rutting activity in the daytime. Still, you can score.

Hang a tree stand or set a ground blind with a commanding view of a cover-laced funnel that leads to or from the last best food source in your area (i.e. a plot of standing corn or leftover acorns). Pray for cold weather and high pressure, which should help pull the survivor bucks out of hiding to feed and perhaps nose for the last estrous does. The darker the moon and the nights, the better your chances of spotting a big deer sneaking around at dawn or dusk.

Forget all you just read if you live and hunt down in Louisiana, Mississippi, Alabama or Texas. For you, the question is: How might a full moon in December or January impact the Southern deer rut?

"It might speed it up by a couple of days, but that's about it," says game-call maker and veteran hunter Will Primos of Jackson, Miss. "Down here, I see days when the moon's phase and position are supposed to be perfect, and we don't see a deer. Other days the moon is supposedly all wrong and we see big bucks running all over the place." Primos plans his hunts around the peak of the rut—December 18, give or take a few days in Mississippi—regardless of moon phase.

Texas outfitter Gary Roberson guides hunters in the Trans-Pecos, where the rut peaks December 1 to 7, and in the south brush country, where deer breed December 7 to 14. How does he adjust when a big moon shines on the prime days?

"I don't change a thing," says Roberson. "In Texas we have so many deer, and they're so tied to feeders in many areas, that the moon doesn't seem to make any difference. When the rut is on, you're gonna see bucks, no matter the phase." Roberson goes on to say that during a full moon, he sometimes sees a flurry of deer activity between 10 A.M. and

2 P.M. That seems to be the one lunar constant from Texas to Saskatchewan.

> **Quick Tip:** Many parts of the country have been hit hard by droughts in recent years, and some meteorologists predict more dry times ahead. When and where there is a lack of rain, keep in mind that many trees drop what mast they produce a month earlier than normal. White oak acorns or other hard or soft mast might have fallen early and been gobbled up by deer and turkeys by the time your bow or gun season rolls around. You'll have to focus on secondary food sources, like honeysuckle and other browse. If much-needed rains come in August or September, the browse will green up and become even more attractive to deer. Look for bucks moving hard and nibbling in thickets.

You Never Know

I once headed to Iowa in mid-December, cramming all the heavy clothes and boots I could find into my duffel. The first afternoon of the hunt, I yanked off my coat, lay back in a ground blind and copped some rays. The sun was bright, the wind blew out of the east and the temperature soared to a record-breaking 58!

At 4 o'clock, 90 minutes before dark, does started piling into the cornfield I was watching. That was not all that surprising; I told you does were pigs, especially late in the season when the rut is done and feed is limited.

Then came the shocker. At 4:10, a giant 9-pointer swaggered out into the field, trotted into a patch of standing corn and started crunching ears. He would score a solid 155! As I eased up my muzzleloader, a doe busted me and flagged away, clearing the field of deer. The buck looked 10 inches larger as he loped away.

It goes to show that nothing—I repeat, nothing—is set in stone. You ought to play the odds with my trigger plan, especially as it relates to hunting around food sources, but you also ought to put in the hours on stand every day you're off work, regardless of weather, moon phase or anything else. You never know really when or where you'll see a big deer on the move.

Chapter 4

Taming the Wind

You can't see it, touch it or even smell it, but your scent is a very tangible thing. As you hike around the woods and climb into and out of tree stands each day, you emit millions upon millions of odiferous molecules into the air. Dead skin, hair oils, nasty gases and sweat-bred bacteria slough off your body. Your clothes, boots, pack and other gear ooze human and chemical odors.

See how this powder floats in the breeze? So do millions of stinky molecules that continuously slough off your skin, hair and gear. Deer can smell that stuff a long way, so clean up your act and learn to play the wind and thermals.

To a whitetail, you're like the Peanuts character Pigpen, forever shrouded in a lingering, stinking fog.

To kill deer, you need to clean up your act (we'll get to that later), but most importantly, you need to play the wind and hunt in spots where your stench is driven away from the legendary noses of does and bucks. In most parts of the country a westerly wind predominates. Which means that many days you can fool bucks simply by setting up somewhere east of food sources, scrapes or bedding areas.

It would be nice if things were that easy. Instead, many mornings and afternoons you'll have to deal with variable winds, unpredictable zephyrs, swirling gusts, rising thermals or downdrafts. You'd better know how to deal with those fickle air currents that spew your scent through the woods and over the plains in many confounding ways.

Light Winds

Whitetails generally move well on days when there's little or no wind and hunters say, "Cool, at least I don't have to worry too much about my scent." Well, think again.

What would happen if you set an open bottle of skunk cover scent in your basement? Pretty soon you'd smell a skunk all over the house. Sit in a tree stand on a windless day, and your scent likewise diffuses. If a buck approaches your stand from virtually any direction, he might smell a rat and spook.

Also, light winds are notorious for kicking up and becoming maddeningly variable, stroking your cheek one minute and lapping the nape of your neck the next. To top things off, when a breeze encounters a tree, ridge top, bluff, copse of thick brush or even a hunter's body in a stand, the resulting turbulence swirls scent particles here, there, and everywhere.

The conventional thinking is that the best way to deal with a finicky breeze is to avoid hunting a spot where a good buck is leaving arm-size rubs and other heavy sign. The theory is that if a big deer winds you in his core area just once, the jig is up. That sounds great on paper, and if you're lucky enough to hunt a large private area all by yourself, it is the way to go.

But most of us share a small woodland or farm with other hunters. Or we hunt public ground that receives moderate to heavy pressure. In either case, I'm a firm believer that you'd better get after a buck while you have him at least partially patterned, even if the wind is light and variable. If you don't risk it once in a while and hunt where a big deer lays down tracks, rubs and scrapes right now, another guy gladly will, either on your property or on a nearby area ... or acorns will dry up ... or a doe a mile away will come into heat. All sorts of things can change a buck's daily routine in the blink of an eye. If you sit home and wait for the perfect wind, "your" buck might leave the area, or egad, another hunter might kill or spook him. Then the jig really will be up.

So I say slip into a scent-control suit, sneak into a spot, hang a couple of stands, grit your teeth and hope for the best. You might get lucky. Think about it. No matter how much you scout, you never really know where a big deer will show up in the woods, especially when he's rutting. He might come from a western thicket one day, from an oak ridge to the north the next, and so on. Don't outthink yourself. How do you really know which wind is best for hunting a stand all the time? The best you can hope for is that a good deer shows up in a spot where a variable wind is at least passable at your stand at the moment of truth.

Use a wind-checker every 20 minutes or so on stand. If you see the breeze or thermals switch big time, move before a big deer comes in and busts you. Don't blow it in your best spot!

You should use a wind-checking device a lot, and it's doubly important when hunting on a risky breeze. Every 20 minutes or so on stand, squeeze a few puffs of white powder, or cut loose a few feathery wind floaters. Study the powder or feathery puffs as they drop, waft and curl away through the woods. You might see that the wind is pretty good until, say, 30 yards from the front of your stand, where it then turns and swirls left, shooting your scent in that direction. That's knowledge you need. If a buck comes in, you know to draw your bow and shoot before he gets tight to the left side of a trail or scrape where he'll smell your swirling scent and spook.

Heavy Winds

I hate it when the wind kicks up to 10 mph or more. Bucks still move reasonably well, but you can't hear them coming in the fallen leaves. The sound of hooves really revs my engine! However, from a scent-control perspective, there are advantages to hunting in a moderate to even a stiff breeze.

For starters, you can use a wind checker or simply stick a wetted finger in the air and discern with reasonable certainty where and how your scent stream is rocketing though the woods or over a plain. You can then hang a stand or take a ground blind with the wind cutting your face or quartering over your shoulder and feel fairly confident that a buck cannot smell you if he approaches out front or off to either side. Also, since your scent is driven in a relatively narrow plume behind you, a deer that angles in slightly downwind might not bust you. Finally, the stronger and steadier the wind, the more your scent stream breaks up when it's tossed against trees, rocks, ridges and other terrain features. When the molecules explode and dissipate, it's difficult for a deer to pin-point your location.

One day, swaying in a tree in a wind-roiled woodlot in Kansas, I cut my eyes to a buck in limbo 150 yards away. I eased up my binocular and watched him closely; only his black-tipped nose moved. The deer worked the wind for a good 10 minutes, whiffing bits and pieces of my scent, but he was not able to pin me down. Finally the jittery buck decided to skulk away to some heavy cover, which just happened to be on the opposite side of my stand. He crossed 50 yards out, within cake range of my muzzleloader. The moderate wind actually helped me score that afternoon.

Morning Thermals

Research shows that mature bucks move best at dusk. Still, I like to hunt a big deer from a morning stand well downwind of thick cover, especially during the rut. When the sun comes up, rising currents of warm air, or thermals, carry your scent particles up, up and away. Who cares if they swirl around in a light to moderate wind? They'll be well above a big deer's sniffer if he shows between 7 to 10 A.M.

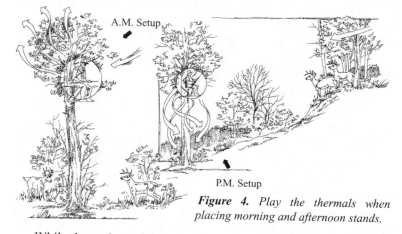

Figure 4. *Play the thermals when placing morning and afternoon stands.*

While thermals work in your favor most of the time, they can blow up in your face if you hunt too low in the mornings. Never let warm, rising air carry your scent up and across a hillside, trail, scrape line or thicket where you expect deer to appear. As a rule, the higher you hunt on a ridge, flat or bluff, the better off you are.

As a sunny day wears on, thermals elevate into what meteorologists call "valley winds." Air heated by the earth rises and moves up valleys, hollows and canyons. Keep hunting high throughout mid-afternoon, watching for deer approaching out of your scent stream below.

Your wind-checker might show no discernible breeze in one spot but squeeze it again 100 yards up a ridge and the powder might swirl and blow hard in one direction. Keep checking the wind as you move in and hang a bow stand.

Dusk Flows

One October day, I discovered an oak flat littered with big tracks, rubs and scrapes. I hadn't seen the buck that was hitting the acorns, but all that sign pointed to a good one. I slipped into the woods after lunch and ran my climber up a tree. Four hours later a doe tipped out of a thicket dead upwind. Perfect! Figuring she was leading a deer parade, I stood up and readied my bow.

Forty yards out the old doe flinched, wheezed and wheeled back the way she came. She stood in the thicket and blew and blew for 10 minutes. Don't you hate it when they do that? Anyway, all I could figure was that the doe had walked in, sniffed the front edge of my scent pool and spooked. All her wheezing alerted every deer within a quarter-mile, blowing up my hunt for the big buck.

As the temperature cools in late afternoon, the air sinks and hovers in a dome just off the ground. This "dusk flow" is a nightmare for the tree-stand hunter. It draws your scent molecules earthward, where they collect in an ever-widening pool. The longer you sit in a stand, the bigger your scent puddle gets. If a deer walks in from any direction, even upwind, and pokes its nose into the pool, you're liable to get busted.

© Charles J. Alsheimer

The longer you sit in a stand, the larger your scent pool can get. If a buck comes in and sticks his nose in the quagmire, this is what you'll see next!

So what are you going to do, never hunt in the evening again? Well, of course not! Slip into a charcoal-activated suit, and spray on an odor neutralizer to minimize the scent cells that draft and pool toward the ground. Again, take a risk and hunt a buck! And whenever possible, use what meteorologists call "mountain breezes" to your advantage.

Modern Gear Tip: I hesitate to say that if you wear a charcoal-activated, scent-absorbing suit, whitetails will never smell you again. But I can say this: I've worn a suit of ScentBlocker Plus (www.robinsonoutdoors.com) hundreds of days in tree stands and ground blinds across the country, and I've had noticeably fewer deer, especially those wary old does, bust me than in seasons past. ScentBlocker pants, jackets, gloves and head nets are available in Mossy Oak Break-Up camouflage. The garments are soft, quiet, lightweight and even water resistant.

As the sun sets each day in autumn and winter, slopes lose heat, and the air cools rapidly. Dense, chilly air slides down hillsides and ridges and into the bottoms of valleys, ridges and canyons. If the buck sign is there, try setting up downwind and slightly below a feeding area, rub line, primary scrape, etc. A mountain breeze should push your scent pool down and away from incoming deer.

Convection Currents

Ever sat in a tree stand and felt air rotating steadily around you? I'm not talking about a variable wind, but a full-blown "convection current." According to meteorologists, when two land masses—say a sunny hillside that slopes into a shady creek bottom—are heated unequally, the air above them becomes turbulent. The warm air on the slope is lighter than the cool air in the bottom. The dense, chilly air drafts toward the ground, lifting the warm air up, where it spreads, cools and falls to complete the convection cycle. The circular flow continues as long as the ridge and bottom remain heated unequally by the sun.

For the hunter, here's what it means. If you sit in the middle of a convection current, your scent stream is in constant

Quick tip: Looking for an au naturel cover scent? Grind your boots in fresh deer droppings as you hike into a stand or blind. If you walk beside a cedar or pine tree, break off a couple of boughs and rub them all over your camouflage clothes.

motion. That sweeping arc of stinky molecules is apt to spook deer coming from any direction. It makes sense, then, not to take an afternoon stand at a point where two terrains are affected in different ways by the sun. A better strategy is to hunt either on a warm, sunny slope or deep in a cool, shady bottom where the wind and vertical air flows are a little more predictable.

It's just another good way to control the scent gremlins in whitetail country.

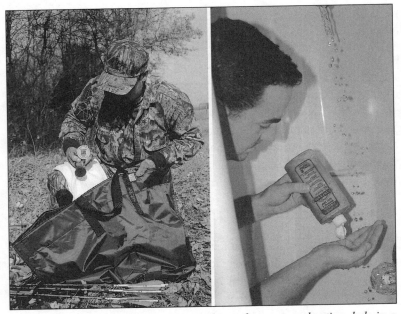

Shower with an odor-killing soap everyday and store your hunting duds in a scent-proof bag. Every little bit helps.

Coming Clean

I once spent a couple of weeks in a primitive tent camp deep in the Canadian bush. By the fourth day, I could smell myself. On the seventh day, I reeked. On the 10th morning of the hunt I slipped within 50 yards of a 165-inch 10-pointer and nailed him with my 30-06.

Quick Tip: Be especially careful when scouting, hanging a tree stand or hunting on a warm day with high humidity. In my experience, that is when whitetails are most apt to smell you. Under those conditions and with a light, variable wind, I don't risk hunting my best spots. I wait until the wind is just right. If the air cools and the humidity drops overnight, that's better yet.

It goes to show that if you play the wind and thermals smartly, you can kill a buck no matter how badly you stink. But it obviously helps to clean up your act:

- Shower and shampoo with unscented soap before each hunt. Dry with an unscented towel. Use an odor-neutralizing deodorant and body powder.
- Brush your teeth with baking soda. Afterwards, try not to eat, smoke or chew tobacco.
- Launder your clothes—underwear, socks, camouflage and everything—in an odor-killing detergent. Line dry outside and store garments in scent-safe bags until you're ready to hunt.
- Wear rubber boots or new leather boots lined with Scent-Lok or Supprescent. I love the latter because your feet don't sweat.
- Spray cotton or fleece Mossy Oak clothes with an odor neutralizer. Don't forget to juice your pack, stand seat, safety harness, pull-up rope, etc.
- The more you sweat, the more you stink. Sneak slowly toward a stand.
- Touch as little brush as possible on the hike to a stand. This cuts the odds that a buck will cruise by and whiff your lingering man-smell an hour or two later.

Chapter 5

Modern Scent Tricks

We mentioned previously that the whitetail's sense of smell is legendary. But do you realize just how awesome a buck's nose is? Get this. Studies have shown that deer are 4000 to 10,000 times more sensitive to odors than we are. Furthermore, scientists say the animals have millions of tiny receptors in their nostrils, which they use to pick up and sort out up to six smells at one time.

Doe-in-heat lure far outsells all other scents combined, but dousing a wick with buck urine or tarsal can be as effective or better for attracting a big buck during the rut.

We already talked about how to clean up your act and play the wind in defense of a deer's olfactory capabilities. Now let's go on offense with some innovative scent tricks designed to take full advantage of a buck's superior snout.

Mist the Air

The conventional way has always been to hang a scent wick 2 to 4 feet off the ground near your tree stand or blind, so that your doe or buck lure disperses, floats and swirls in the wind. Well, keep doing that, and then take things a step further. Climb into your stand and every once in a while, pull out a pump-bottle of doe lure and mist the air so that it floats downwind. You might even spray the backside of the tree you're sitting in occasionally. It will keep your lure super-active throughout a hunt.

Proof positive that a tarsal wick works. One November morning this buck came to smell an "intruder" and gave me a great photo op. Hang your wicks high so the breeze will carry and swirl the scent far through the woods.

Stink Some Dirt

These days hunters are having some great luck with ground scents, like smoking sticks that release a sexual lure; time-release beads that activate doe scent for days; estrus powders; and real droppings collected from hot does. There are even contraptions that heat and vaporize a lure and send it wafting up from the ground and down through the woods.

If you're not having much success with airborne scents, you might as well try stinking up some dirt. Do it during the hard pre-rut in late October or early November (or mid-December or mid-January down

Knight & Hale's pop-open scent canisters and spikes are convenient to carry and use. No fuss, no muss!

South). Sprinkle powder or beads or light a stick to build a scent-post near your tree stand or blind. Or, better yet, doctor a real scrape's dirt nearby. Check the Cabela's or Bass Pro catalog for a wide range of ground scents.

Scent a Trail

One of the best spots for hot-doe lure is on the upwind side of a deer trail. That way, the lure blows down and across the path. If a buck comes along, either on the trail or in cover downwind of it, he should smell the stuff. There's a good chance he'll stop, raise his nose and try to sort out the sweet aroma. If your stand or blind is in the right spot, a little further downwind of the trail, you might get a shot. Try to hang your pads or wicks out of direct sun and in the shade. The scent will remain cool and moist and permeate the trail and surrounding cover for hours.

Stink Like a Buck

One November morning I drilled a good buck and walked up to him. Man, he stunk! His hind legs and hocks were wet and black from rub-urinating in scrapes all night long. I held my breath and started gutting. Then I heard popping in the leaves. I looked up and saw a 10-pointer, much larger than the deer I had just shot, bearing down on me! His rack was poised for battle and the hair bristled on his swollen neck.

I shivered and hid behind the dead buck, not really knowing what to do. A rut-crazed animal like that is unpredictable and potentially dangerous, and I figured staying put was my best bet. Anyway, the intruder

This buck reeked more than any other deer I have ever shot. As I dressed him, his tarsal stench lured a bigger 10-pointer into the area. It was a little scary but awesome to experience.

marched within 10 yards, grunting and giving me the evil eye. When my deer didn't pose a threat, the big bad dude whirled and trotted off. It was an awesome and scary experience, and it taught me a lot.

Now, during the last days of the scraping phase and just before the bucks start chasing in early November here in Virginia, I set a witch's brew of buck urine and tarsal scent near my tree stands. Sometimes I make scent-posts in the dirt, other times I hang juiced wicks. It all depends on the terrain and wind direction where I'm hunting. You should know that strong-smelling tarsal might scare off young bucks. But every once in a while, it will pull in a mature, aggressive deer looking for a challenge. In my experience, the rank stuff works better than doe lure in the days immediately preceding the peak of the rut.

Scent Traps

I also use buck urine or tarsal when rattling and grunting late in the pre-rut. I soak boot pads and lay a rutting-buck trail into a calling site. Then I walk around my stand a couple of times. I hang the pads, or wicks misted with fresh buck juice on a tree limb to either side of my stand and 20 to 50 yards downwind.

It stinks where I call, and that's the way I like it. When a buck responds to rattling or aggressive tending grunts, he expects to smell other deer. Many times a big deer will circle downwind of your calling to sniff out what he thinks is a buck fight or an intruder tending a doe. That's why the scent-posts are out there. I want a buck to smell them and stop or approach before he gets dead downwind and busts me.

Steal a Stick

An old-timer taught me an unusual trick years ago, and I've added it my modern routine. Look for an active buck scrape a couple of miles from where you hunt. Pull on a pair of rubber surgical gloves, pull out your saw or hand clipper and steal the scrape's mangled "lick branch." Pack that stick into your hunting spot and tie it to a limb upwind of your tree stand. Then paw a mock scrape beneath it. Juice the dirt with buck urine and tarsal, and maybe sprinkle some hot-doe drops nearby. There's no faking it here. That lick branch is the real deal, and it just might fool a buck that comes in to smell an intruder in his domain.

Juice a Decoy

In the right situation, a doe or buck decoy can pull a buck close to your stand or blind. I've also seen a fake deer scare the wits out of whitetails. You just never know.

Most of the time a buck will circle downwind to check out a decoy. Well, give him something to smell. If you use a fake doe, raise its tail and smear estrus lure on it. If you stake out a bogus buck, doctor it with tarsal scent. The sight and smell of your imposter might be too much for a buck to resist. If one comes in, shoot as soon as you get a good opportunity. In my experience the closer a deer comes to a decoy, the more tense and spookier it gets. At any moment, regardless of what he smells, a buck is apt to turn tail, flag off 50 yards, stop and look back as if to ask, "What the heck is that?"

Grand Central Signpost

Says Kentucky call maker and whitetail authority David Hale, "If you're lucky, someday you'll find what I call a 'central signpost,' a rub as thick as your leg. Look close and you'll see four, five or more healed scars, so you know the local bucks have rubbed that tree for years." Hale theorizes that a huge rub is like a community scrape. "I believe most every deer that walks within a quarter-mile of it will veer over to smell it and maybe rub forehead scent on it," he says. "Deer are naturally attracted to a signpost, or at least to the cover that surrounds it, so it gives you a good spot to start hunting."

Scout out from a giant rub for a trail pocked with fresh buck tracks and rimmed with smaller rubs and maybe some scrapes. Then set doe or buck urine upwind of the trail in hopes of enticing the resident big boy and stopping him for a shot.

The Ultimate Scent Trail

Park your truck, douse a couple of boot pads with fox or skunk scent, and take off down through the woods or over a prairie. When you're about 200 yards from a spot you plan to hunt, remove the pads, tie a drag rag to your boot, soak it with hot-doe lure and sneak the rest of the way in. You might want to make a couple of big sweeps around your stand. A buck that comes from any direction might cut the scent and circle in to see what's up.

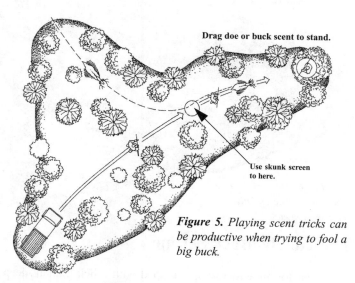

Drag doe or buck scent to stand.

Use skunk screen to here.

Figure 5. *Playing scent tricks can be productive when trying to fool a big buck.*

"If you lay a doe trail all the way in from your truck to your stand, a buck might cut it, turn the wrong way and end up back at your vehicle," notes Don Bell, president of the Code Blue scent company. "When you switch scents halfway in, you know a buck is not gonna follow your fox scent. But he might turn toward the doe scent and follow it right to your stand."

I bet you never thought of that. I sure hadn't until Bell filled me in, but it makes a lot of sense.

One Last Trail

Speaking of laying down a scent trail ... most hunters do it only in the pre-rut and into the peak, but you ought to try it during the first few days of the post-rut as well. "Mature bucks still have that breeding desire, and they cruise around in search of the last hot does," says Steve Stoltz, a St. Louis firefighter who archery hunts big whitetails across the Midwest. "The best part about it is that late in the season there aren't many hot does left in most areas. If a buck hits your estrus trail, he might get excited and follow it in."

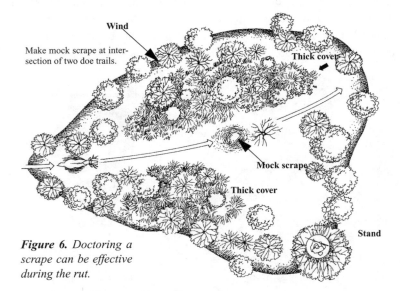

Figure 6. Doctoring a scrape can be effective during the rut.

The Timely Mock Scrape

Scout for an active scrape, topped with a lick branch, deep in the woods and on the edge of a thicket where old bucks love to travel. Hide a portable stand in a nearby tree—30 yards away if archery hunting, and a good 75 to 100 yards away if hunting with a muzzleloader, shotgun or centerfire rifle. Then go to work on the scrape in a timely manner.

One afternoon around 4:30 or 5:00, sneak in and freshen the scrape with tarsal scent. Spread a little hot-doe scent in the area while you're at it. A dominant buck might come along that night, get mad as hell, rip up the scrape and rub-urinate in it. Go back the next afternoon at 4:30 or 5:00 and doctor the scrape again. The buck might come back that night and rip it up once more. Keep it up for several days, freshening the scrape at the same time every afternoon. Pretty soon the buck might want to see or encounter the intruder putting down all that rank scent, so he might come and check the scrape earlier and earlier each night. You might get a crack at him one evening from that stand you hunt close by.

Mock Rubs

If bucks haven't already done it, I often blaze a couple of rubs near a natural or mock scrape I'm watching. Use a saw or wood rasp to strip the bark off a couple of thick trees (make sure it's legal if you hunt on public ground). Rub like an aggressive buck—scar the trees 2 to 3 feet off the ground, and snap some low-hanging branches. Lather your mock rubs with special forehead scent, or use regular old buck urine. Depending on the terrain and wind conditions, a buck might see or smell your shiny new rubs 50 to 100 yards out and circle into the scrape you're hunting and give you a shot.

Try blazing a mock rub with a saw or wood rasp, and smear some buck scent on it. A big deer might come along, see the rub and come in to investigate the fake scrape you built nearby.

Modern Gear Tip: On a rainy or snowy day, try one of the new gel lures. Smear a gob of doe or buck scent on a wick, branch or the side of a tree near your stand. It won't evaporate, wash away or freeze as quickly as a liquid lure might.

Scent Talk

Toss these terms around and impress your hunting buddies:

Flehmening (a.k.a. lip curling): A mature buck tracks a doe to a spot where she recently urinated. He licks or inhales the pee, lays back his head and lip curls. Scientists say the vomeronasal organ in the roof of the mouth helps a buck analyze the scent in the urine to determine a doe's state of estrus. If the pee smells right, the buck will continue to track the doe.

A mature buck often circles through cover downwind of a trail, and then lip curls to check the estrus state of does that wander by.

© Charles J. Alsheimer

Pheromones: These chemical substances produced by deer in their gland secretions and urine serve as stimuli to other deer for behavioral responses. Conventional wisdom says pheromones given off by does drive bucks crazy and start the peak-breeding phase. But some biologists now suggest that pheromones emitted by bucks as they rub and scrape stimulate does into estrus. Their exact role is up in the air, but pheromones are undoubtedly important in the breeding ritual.

Quick Tip: Is that bottle of doe or buck urine you bought last fall still steaming for this season? If you didn't open it, and if you stored it in a cool, dark place, it should be okay. But you probably carried the lure in your daypack and used it a few times. Sunlight, air and heat likely broke down and ammoniated the urine. Toss it and buy a fresh bottle.

Rub-urination: Rutting bucks rub their hind legs together and pee over their hocks into scrapes and along doe trails. As the urine mixes with tarsal scent and cakes on their legs, bucks start to stink. If you're downwind, you can smell a rutting buck for 100 yards or more. A buck's rank scent can linger on a ridge or in a bottom for hours, especially if he beds there. Hang a stand where you smell a rutting buck, and set a heavy dose of tarsal scent nearby. There's a decent chance that stinky buck will come looking for the intruder.

I watched this buck lick and chew limbs every 20 yards along a trail, even though there were no scrapes beneath the branches. I figured he was depositing salivary scent and leaving his calling card for does and other bucks.

Salivary Scent: The more I watch rutting bucks, the more I'm convinced their saliva plays a huge role in communication. After rubbing trees, deer sometimes lick them. Bucks also chew and lick limbs above scrapes. One day I watched a big 8-pointer approach a feeding area. He paused every 20 yards to lick low-lying limbs, even though there were no scrapes beneath them. My interpretation was that the buck was leaving his calling card for does and other bucks.

Chapter 6

Real-World Deer Calling

I don't care what any call maker tells you about his hottest new gizmo. I don't care how much incredible video footage you see of giant bucks bounding in to rattling horns, or strolling within feet of hunters piping on grunt tubes or bleat calls. The truth is, most days calling just doesn't work.

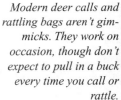

Modern deer calls and rattling bags aren't gimmicks. They work on occasion, though don't expect to pull in a buck every time you call or rattle.

Ah, but before I get too negative on you, let me say this: If you hang tough and rattle or grunt every day for a month this fall, and if you time things right during the rut, you *will* strike a chord with a few bucks. One day an old 8- or 10-pointer might like what he hears and come looking for you. Shoot him, tag him and make your season. That's deer calling in the real world.

Rattling

Whacking a set of antlers falls under a secondary definition of "call" in *Webster's Tenth*: "to command or request to come." By mimicking two deer tangling with their racks, you might command a buck to your stand, be it an inquisitive youngster or an old bruiser looking for rivals battling over a hot doe.

Rattling was originated in Texas some 50 years ago, and down there it keeps on producing awesome results. On the intensively managed ranches where the buck-to-doe ratio is at or near 1:1, there's keen competition among the 3 ½- to 6 ½-year-old bucks for the favors of the few does. When the rut is on in December, you can cruise around a ranch, crack your horns from several different spots and expect five, 10, maybe even 20 or 30 bucks to bound in each day.

I prefer to rattle from the ground on still, frosty mornings late in the pre-rut and into the peak. The technique works best for me from sunrise till 10:00 A.M.

But that is Texas. If you hunt anywhere else in North America—where the buck-to-doe ratio is not so balanced, where there are fewer mature bucks per square mile and where the hunting pressure in not so tightly controlled—things are different. Big-time different! You aren't going to rattle up 10 bucks a day, or even five. Heck, you probably won't command that many bucks to your stand all season. But you might rattle in one or two if you go about it right.

You might have heard that the early pre-rut (mid-October in most places) is a good time to "spar," or to tick and grind a set of horns to simulate bucks horsing around and testing each other's dominance. The theory is that by sparring every once in a while on stand, you might pull in a curious buck. Well, years ago, I used to spar quite a lot, but no more.

One October afternoon a few years ago, I was bowhunting in Montana, hoping to nail a good buck on film for a TV show. My stand was on the edge of an alfalfa field, which filled up with deer an hour before dusk. Thirty does and 15 bucks, eight of them legitimate P&Y candidates, streamed past just out of shooting range. They walked out to the middle of the field and began feeding 200 to 300 yards away.

"I'm gonna do a little sparring and try to pull one of those bucks over here," I whispered to my cameraman. The video whirred as I ticked and grinded the horns lightly.

Every deer in the field threw up its head and then its tail and ran! Now there's some incredible footage you'll never see on TV. More than 40 deer and a bunch of P&Y bucks running like hell *away* from an "expert's" rattling.

Reflecting on that hunt, I got to thinking, *How many deer have I spooked like that over the past 20 years?* Mostly I'd sparred in the thick woods back East and down South. I'm sure many bucks that I could not see in the timber had heard me and bolted or at least eased out of an area because I hadn't timed my calling right.

Now I rarely work the horns until deep in the pre-rut—late October or early November in most places, and mid to late December or January in the Deep South. For 10 days or so before the main wave of mature does comes into heat, bucks go on the prowl, rubbing and scraping and throwing some of their caution to the wind. That, my friend, is the time to rattle. Sparring or even all-out mock battles shouldn't intimidate bucks. To the contrary, the natural rutting sounds might pull in a big deer looking to watch or join a brawl.

I read one time where your initial rattling volley should be just right: Crack the horns, grind them for a few seconds, make a clean break and repeat the routine. Phooey! All buck racks are unique. Some are massive while others are spindly. A deer might have seven, eight or 10 points, and the tines might be long and thin or short and thick. So when two dudes tangle, how do you know exactly what sounds their antlers will make? You don't. Also, all buck fights vary in intensity and duration.

The fact is there is no right or wrong way to rattle. Just do what feels right, within reason, each day. I typically spar horns or work a rattle bag moderately hard in 30- to 60-second bursts. Sometimes, I hammer a set of real or synthetic antlers for a minute or two. Hunting from the ground, I thrash bushes, rake leaves and pound a horn on the ground to mimic the foot stamping of an irate buck. If I'm in a tree stand, I whack the side of the tree hard a few times before or after a rattling sequence. Man, a buck can hear those cracks a mile away!

When a buck responds, he looks hard for two bucks fighting. Don't let him see you. Wear your Mossy Oak, a facemask and gloves, and don't fidget around too much.

Some people will tell you that once the rut explodes, you might as well hang up your horns. After all, there's no way you're going to rattle a big buck off the tail of the hot doe he is chasing or tending, right? There is merit to that, but I keep on rattling anyway. Plenty of sexually frustrated "beta" bucks roam the woods, and one of them might very well come racing in to investigate your calls. While he might be a subdominant buck, he might be 3-½ years old, with an 8- or 10-point rack that tapes 130 inches or more. Wouldn't you like to tag him? And who knows, you might even rattle up a dominant, sex-crazed whopper that is between does and looking to mix things up.

You ought to keep rattling right on into the first week of the post-rut as well. Actually, this is one of today's best-kept secrets. Hunters across the country and particularly in the Midwest are rattling in some huge bucks in late November and even early December. One reason is that due to recent weather patterns, the days are often much cooler than they were back in late October or early November. So deer naturally move better.

Couple that with the fact that for a week to 10 days after the major breeding period is over, mature bucks that survive hunting season stay on the prowl for does. As compared to 3 weeks ago, there are far fewer receptive gals roaming the woods and plains now. If a big deer hears what he perceives to be two rivals battling over one of the fall's last hot does, he might lay back his ears, raise his hackles and zoom in for a look. Now that would cap your season with a bang, guaranteed!

Grunt Calling

Does and young bucks pipe high-pitched grunts while mature males talk deep and gutturally. That seems to be the consensus with most hunters and biologists I talk to.

Well, they are sometimes right, but I've heard many old bucks with nasal, wimpy grunts. Tons of spikes and 4-pointers have trotted beneath my tree stands grunting like market hogs during the rut. So you never really know.

Grunt at every buck you see cruising just out of bow range. If a deer hears your calls, most of the time he'll stop, and he might turn your way.

When you blow a grunt tube, your goal is to simply sound like a deer. But you ought to mix it up and blow both trilling and throaty grunts throughout your time on stand. Who knows which sound will appeal to a buck that might cruise by in the cover? He may like the deep stuff, or the trilling sounds.

Early in the pre-rut, or later in the post-rut for that matter, you have nothing to lose by blowing a few "contact grunts" throughout the morning or afternoon. Huff air up from your diaphragm and into a tube to make calls that sound like *ecc, ecc* or *urk, urk, urk*. On stand, string together three or four sets of grunts every 15, 20 or 30 minutes. The idea is to contact a buck and hopefully reel him in.

As the rut approaches, bucks become more brazen and vocal, and so should you. Blow quick, choppy series of "aggression" or "tending grunts" to mimic a buck prowling for a doe or dogging her or herding her into cover for some fun. The calls should sound something like *urrrp, urrrp, urrrp* or *urrrg, urrrg, urrrg*. Five- to 10-second sequences are most realistic, but grunt longer if you like. Sometimes a buck with a hot doe in sight will utter and hold a "clicking grunt" for 15 to 20 seconds. Again, like rattling, basically anything goes. A wild, horny buck may come to what he thinks is a rival tending a hot doe or an interloper cruising for a bruising.

Every once in a while you might get lucky with "blind grunting" from a stand or blind. But without a doubt, grunting is most effective after you see a buck. Let's say you spot a big deer cresting a ridge, slipping down a funnel or flashing through cover just out of bow range. Don't just sit there. Grunt! If the deer hears you, and he should from 100 yards or farther on a calm day, most of the time he'll stop and look. If you're gun hunting, that might be the only break you need.

If a buck stops for a second but continues walking (which is actually what happens most of the time) grunt again, a little bit louder. And if you can get away with it, you might even ease up your rattling horns or bag and do some ticking and grinding. A combination of grunting and rattling can be the ticket that turns a rutting buck your way.

Bleating

An estrous doe is fussy, and in deer speak her sassy bleats—*meaaaa, meaaaa*—say to a buck, "Hey big boy, I'm over here and ready for some loving!" In 25 years of hunting, I think I've heard this call 10 times in the woods. But many times, especially around feeding areas, I've heard does utter softer bleats—*mea, mea*.

Call maker Will Primos makes 3 estrus bleats on his CAN and follows up with grunts to simulate a hot breeding scenario.

Will Primos is a big fan of bleating. He sometimes backs up a series of bleats with an aggravated doe snort or two. "It's not the foot-stamping danger snorts that you hear, but more of a general blowing or wheezing that deer make on the move," says the Mississippi game call maker. "If a doe is not ready to breed, she'll often blow at a buck. I think other bucks listen for that, and sometimes they'll come to check it out." Other days Primos makes three estrous doe bleats followed by two short grunts and then two more estrous bleats to mimic a hot breeding scenario.

Many of today's grunt tubes can be adjusted for bleating, but the hottest bleat call going these days is the cylindrical CAN from Primos Hunting Calls. The CAN works on the same principle as the old turn-over toy that sounded like a mooing cow. Simply turn the can upside down in your hand to bleat like a doe. It couldn't hurt to try it sometime. Biologists recognize twelve whitetail vocalizations. You never know which one—maybe the bleat—may strike a chord with a buck.

Grunt-Snort-Wheeze

The grunt-snort-wheeze—which sounds sort of like *pfft, pfft, pff-teeeezzzzzee*—has been getting some ink recently. Biologists and experienced hunters point out that the call is by far the most aggressive one in the whitetail's vocabulary. "You can use the grunt-snort-wheeze to bring in a dominant deer during the rut, but it can also scare off some bucks," says noted whitetail researcher Dr. Karl Miller of the University of Georgia.

Mark Drury developed a grunt-snort-wheeze tube a few years ago. The aggressive call might pull in a dominant buck during the rut, but it can also spook young bucks.

Terry Drury, whose brother, Mark, designed a grunt-snort-wheeze call for the M.A.D. call company, agrees. "It can and will scare off immature bucks, but it can also produce dramatic results," says Terry. "We think the call is a mature buck's warning signal. He won't tolerate subordinate bucks in his area during the rut, so he grunt-snort-wheezes at them. Sometimes the call drives a big deer crazy."

One November afternoon the Drury boys spotted an old 7-pointer chasing does and running off young bucks in a cornfield. The 150-inch deer was obviously the king, even though he had one less point than the other bucks in the area. Anyhow, the old deer ducked into a thicket with a doe. Terry rattled. The big 7 popped out, looked and went back to his gal.

"I figured what the heck, so I grunt-snort-wheezed," recalls Terry. "The buck ran out of the cover and to within 30 yards of our stands," says Mark, who was filming Terry's hunt that day. "The deer turned to leave, and Terry called again. The buck trotted below our tree and ripped a scrape. It was awesome."

Don't expect such dramatic results every time you try it, but the grunt-snort-wheeze is worth a shot on occasion, especially if you hunt private, managed ground with a good age-structure of mature bucks. Every deer I've seen snort-wheeze in the woods or on a video stamps its foot like crazy as it utters the call. If you're on the ground, mimic that and pop your fist or a rattling horn in the leaves as you blow the call.

Location, Location

Calling whitetails is like running a business. Set up in a bad part of town and you'll go bankrupt. But work in the right location, in a spot where you'll get a lot of walk-through customers, and you can strike it rich. Try these six sets to cash in on bucks:

In the mornings, set up to rattle and grunt downwind of woods thickets, swamps and similar bedding covers.

1. **Broken country:** A rut-crazed buck might charge across a crop field or grassland to check out your rattles, snort-wheezes or guttural grunts—it happens all the time down in Texas. But in most parts of the country, I believe you're better off setting up in brushy woodlands or "broken" spotty or linear cover, where a big deer feels most comfortable working in to your sounds.

2. **Timber thickets:** I like to rattle and grunt downwind of deep-woods thickets, swamps and similar security covers in the mornings. I find that rattling in particular works best in the a.m.

3. **Food sources:** In the afternoons, I typically don't rattle much around food sources. But I grunt and/or bleat around mast flats, clover plots and crop fields where the does and bucks are coming to feed.

4. **Funnels:** Sometimes, especially when gun hunting, it pays to set up and call where you can watch a big chunk of country. Does on the brink of estrus run draws, hollows and the brushy edges of creeks and rivers every day (the more fresh buck sign in a funnel, the better). Where hot does travel and drip scent, horny bucks are sure follow. And the more ground you can see, the better the chance that you'll spot a cruiser buck. Use sharp rattling or the grunt-snort-wheeze to reach out and touch a deer in a funnel or bottom. Then try to reel him close with sparring or grunts.

5. **Ridges:** Try calling on high ground laced with brush, honeysuckle or similar cover. Many bucks bed and travel in and around ridge thickets, so you're in good position to start with. Also, you

should have a good view of funnels, flats or fields below. The kicker: The wind and thermals are normally fairly steady and predictable on a ridge, so if you set up smartly, deer are less apt to smell you. Bucks like to work the steady winds as they prowl around and scent-check for does, so it's a perfect scenario to strike 'em with rattles, grunts or bleats.

6. **Barriers:** Whenever possible put some type of terrain barrier 50 to 100 yards behind your tree stand or ground blind. Some examples: a thick windrow, a river, a steep buff or a fenced pasture. Mature bucks like to circle downwind to get a whiff of fighting or grunting deer. If you can block a buck with a barrier, you force him to approach your calls from the side or out front where he can't wind you and spook, which means he'll be easier to see and shoot.

Are Bucks Getting Call Shy?

Grunting and rattling are two of the hottest modern tactics of deer hunters across North America. To me it begs the questions: Are bucks getting call shy? Will they ever?

Most of the biologists and expert hunters I've spoken with do not believe bucks will ever turn a deaf ear to grunt or bleat calls. Rattling is another matter.

Kentucky call maker and whitetail authority Harold Knight does not believe bucks will shy from the actual sounds of two deer fighting. But he says, "Suppose one day you rattle in a big deer. The buck comes in and doesn't see two bucks fighting. Or worse, he sees you moving around or smells you. That buck certainly might be leery to come to more rattling in the area for the rest of the season."

Dan Perez, who works for PSE Archery and bowhunts trophy deer across the Midwest, spins it this way: "With so many hunters rattling in the timber these days, I believe mature bucks learn that too much rattling is unrealistic," he says. "For that reason, I rattle a little differently than most hunters. I might climb into a stand and rattle hard for two minutes, then not rattle again for two hours. In my opinion, the first time a mature buck hears rattling, he knows exactly where it came from. He may eventually work his way in if you don't scare him with more rattling or too much movement."

Quick tip: Fiddling with a grunt tube can cost you a shot when a buck is close and moving fast. Stop him with your voice—a simple *ecc* or *urp* should do the trick. Make sure to draw your bow or point your gun at a deer *before* you make a peep.

Calling Pointers

- Bucks that come to rattling or calling look hard for the sources of those sounds. Wear Mossy Oak head to toe, including gloves and a face-mask. Top off with a blaze orange vest for safety during gun season.

> **Modern Gear Tip:** I've tested hundreds of grunt calls over the years, and most of them sound enough like a deer to work. But my all-time favorite remains Knight & Hale's EZ Grunter Plus, which is great for either soft or aggressive calling. Get you one and use it … Some people say bucks can tell the "ping" of synthetic antlers. Hogwash! I've rattled in a bunch of bucks with synthetics. Primos' Fightin' Horns, which are well balanced and have six perfectly molded grinding tines, work great.

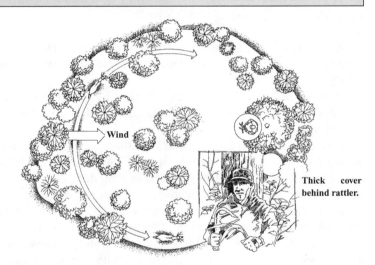

Figure 7. Pay attention to your setup when rattling for big bucks.

- Set up with the sun at your back and against thick cover. You'll be hidden in the shadows, and an incoming buck will be easy to see if sunlight flashes on his antlers or hide. Also, you need to trick a buck into thinking deer are fighting, tending or breeding in the brush 50 to 100 yards behind you. That forces him to keep looking, listening and moving, hopefully into bow or gun range.
- After each routine, quietly lay down the horns or call, sit still and scan the cover all around. One thing is certain: Rattling, grunting or bleating won't work if you move around too much and spook bucks that might be on the way in.

Chapter 7

Rise and Shine

I love to sneak around and stalk whitetails with a rifle or even a bow. But I'm a pragmatist, and I know that most days I'm better off perched in a tree.

If you hunt a 20- to 50-acre block of woods, you're generally best off in a tree stand. You don't walk around, spook bucks and drive them off your property. You can see well, and your scent is above deer.

One huge benefit to hunting from a tree stand is that you don't walk around and spook bucks. You don't knock a big deer off his natural pattern, or worse, push him across a fence and into the sights of another hunter waiting on the other side.

Up a tree, your scent and silhouette are above the noses and eyes of deer, another obvious advantage. Up there, you can see well and cover a lot of terrain. Most days you won't shoot a buck, but you will look out and see deer moving on nearby ridges or in fields or funnels. You can and should study the animals and get a read on their most current patterns. Then, if necessary, you can pull your stand, move and rehang it in a hotter spot for a quick-strike meeting with a mature buck.

Your tree-stand success hinges on three factors. In following chapters, you'll find many specific setups for hunting the rut and the early and late seasons. Here we'll focus on the first two important things: How to choose the stand that best suits your style of hunting, and how to hang that perch for a good crack at a buck cruising below.

The Fixed-Position Tree Stand

Modern fixed-position stands from Summit, Ol' Man, and other companies are constructed of either welded steel or aircraft-grade aluminum. As tree stands go, they're compact, lightweight (10 to 20 pounds) and easy to pack into the woods.

A fixed stand can be strapped or chained to virtually any type of tree—large, thin, stunted, straight or crooked. Hung correctly, this type of perch is quiet and solid. The smaller models are easily concealed amid limbs, leaves, vines and the like, reducing the odds of a buck looking up and busting you.

A fixed-position stand can be a bear to hang, but it works great for setting up in either large or small trees with lots of branches.

You should know that a fixed-position stand is no piece of cake to hang. Strapped into a safety harness or climbing belt and teetering on screw-in steps or a ladder, you must rope up a stand, hold it in one hand, reach around a tree, hook a chain or strap to the platform, straighten the stand, then cinch everything down tight. A perch is easy to take down or "pull," but then you have to go to work again to relocate it near a food source, bedding area, scrape or the like.

If you're a stickler for silence in the deer woods, choose a stand that hooks to a tree with a webbed strap (a chain is super-strong, but it is noisy on the hike in and at hang time). Before you buy, examine a platform and make sure it has well-designed teeth or points that will securely bite a tree. This not only makes a stand safe, it also keeps it from sliding a half-inch and popping or squeaking. Since you'll spend hours sitting and waiting for a buck, make sure the stand you choose has a comfortable seat.

A fixed-position stand is an excellent choice if you're relatively young and in good shape, and if you like to hike a half-mile or deeper into the woods and thickets where a lot of the big bucks hang out. Ditto if you're the energetic type who doesn't mind the work of hanging, pulling and relocating stands as deer patterns change. If you hunt an area where large, straight trees are in short supply, a fixed-position stand is the only way to go.

The Climbing Stand

For hunters who live east of the Mississippi River, or in any area with lots of straight hardwood and softwood trees roughly 8 to 20 inches in diameter, a climbing stand works great. Scout out a spot blazed with big rubs, tracks and scrapes. Run your climber up a tree downwind of the sign, and you're hunting the resident buck in minutes. Mobility is a huge advantage. If the wind or deer patterns change, shinny down the tree, pull your stand, put it on your back, do more scouting and climb another tree in a hot area.

Years ago climbing stands were noisy. You could hear a hunter rattling his old Baker up a tree a half-mile away. But today's well-designed stands from Ol' Man, Summit and others allow you to climb trees not only quickly but also quietly.

A two-piece climber weighs 15 to 30 pounds, and it's bulky. A stand's front and side rails can be tight and restrictive, especially when

A climber allows you to stay mobile. After spotting a buck or finding fresh sign, you can move into an area, run your stand up a tree and be hunting in a matter of minutes.

archery hunting. Sometimes it's tough to find a straight tree in a spot you want to hunt. Hiding a climber in a tree, especially late in the season when the leaves are down, can be a problem.

But all in all, if you hunt an area with lots of straight trees, or if you like to move around a lot, a climber is a great choice. Before purchasing a stand, check both seat and foot platforms for well-designed blades that will bite softwood or hardwood trees. Check how the pieces attach to a tree—a stand that requires minimal brace and pin adjustments is best. Make sure the two sections are large enough to fit around trees 20 inches or so in diameter. Check the bottom platform for large, easy-to-adjust "foot holds." The better your boots fit in the straps, the easier and quieter you'll climb a tree.

The Ladder Stand

A ladder stand is easy to strap or chain to a midsize or huge tree, even a slightly crooked one. Once hung, a ladder is easy and safe to climb, and it's the most comfortable stand to sit in for hours.

No way around it—a ladder, with three or four aluminum or steel sections, is heavy and bulky to pack into the woods. It's also the hardest of all the stands to conceal.

A ladder stand is big, heavy and bulky. But it is super-comfortable and my favorite choice for gun hunting.

Still, a ladder can be a good choice for the bow or gun hunter, especially if you like to set a stand on a ridge or overlooking a funnel and then hunt there most of the season. A solid, easy-to-climb ladder is a good choice for a young hunter, or an older hunter with a bad back or a bum knee.

When buying a ladder, make sure it has at least one well-designed stabilizing bar that you ratchet midway up a tree to prevent the stand from swaying and twisting under your weight. Purchase one or two extra ladder sections that will let you hunt at least 16 feet high. If you're a gun hunter, add an optional "sissy bar" that attaches to the stand, encircles your body and provides a solid shooting rest.

Ten Stand-Setting Pointers

1. Don't spook a buck before you hunt him. Before leaving your truck, secure stand sections, seats, chains and buckles with rope or elastic straps so they won't clang around as you hike into a spot.
2. Approach a stand site from a downwind or crosswind angle, and through a "dead zone" where few if any deer hang out. Never walk along a deer trail or fresh scrape line, and try to cut a path in as few places as possible. The fewer deer that see or smell you on the way in, the better off you are.

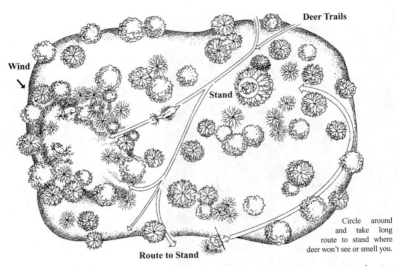

Figure 8. When hunting big bucks, pay close attention to your entry and exit routes.

3. Select a spot where the wind is right, quartering away from a feeding area, thicket or funnel where you expect to see deer. Then back off 100 yards or so and scout the surrounding terrain. Many times you'll find an even better tree for a stand.

4. Once you've chosen a tree, walk all the way around it, looking 15 to 20 feet up to see which angle provides the best backdrop for your perch. Try to conceal a stand amid limbs, leaves or vines. Old does and bucks look up more than ever these days, especially in areas with intense bowhunting pressure. Tucking a fixed-position stand in the fork of a tree or running a climber up to the "Y" helps to hide you.

5. You can see a deer best when sunlight glints on his antlers or hide. Same with a buck—he might bust you if he sees sunlight reflecting off a stand, or glinting on a bow or gun as you move around in a perch. Always try to set a stand in mottled shadows, preferably with the rising or setting sun at your back. You'll be hidden in the shade, and a buck that looks into the sun can't see you. Besides, facing a morning stand west and an evening stand east gives you an extra 10 to 15 minutes of shooting visibility at dawn and dusk.

6. Set a stand as quickly and as quietly as you can. If you're hanging with a buddy, whisper. Don't throw stands and ladder steps around. Any noise can alert a nearby buck to your presence, and it might

Bucks look up more than ever these days, so hide your stand as best you can. Check out how all the limbs and vines break this bowhunter's silhouette. Awesome setup!

cause him to change his pattern just enough so that you never see him in shooting light. You will have gone to a lot of trouble for nothing.

7. Don't just stick a stand on a tree, angle it into the wind so you can draw a bow or aim a gun with little movement when a buck shows. If you're right-handed, set a fixed, climbing or ladder perch where the prevailing breeze hits your left shoulder (vice versa for southpaws).

8. Sometimes it pays to face a stand *opposite* of where you think deer will appear. Putting a tree between you and approaching whitetails provides the optimum cover. If you hear a buck walking behind your stand, sit tight. If he keeps coming and quarters away, glue a sight pin or crosshair behind his shoulder and fire.

9. You can hunt a stand the same day you hang it, especially when using a climber, but in my experience, it is always best to "rest" a fixed-position or ladder stand for a day or two after you hang it.

10. Get organized when you come back to hunt a stand. When you step out of your truck, slip into your safety harness. Sling a binocular around your neck, and tuck it in the top of your jacket. Store bow release, wind checker, pull-up rope, scents and wicks, grunt call and other items in clothes or pack pockets within easy reach. Slip into your perch, climb up and ready your gear in an orderly manner. You'll make less noise and minimize your movements, and your odds of spotting a good buck an hour or so later go way up.

Tree-Stand Accessories

Steps: To climb trees and hang and access fixed-position stands, carry at least 10 screw-in steps, or pack four or five of the new ladder sections into the woods. Ladders are heavier and bulkier, but they're easier and safer to climb. Run screw-in steps or ladder sections a foot *above* a stand. Climb to the very top and step easily and safely down onto the platform.

I prefer ladder sections to screw-in steps for hanging a fixed-position stand. Run the rungs a foot above where you set the perch. When you come back to hunt, climb to the top and sit safely down onto the platform.

Extra steps: Carry a couple of spare steps. Screw them into a tree on either side of a stand, and hang your bow, binocular, rattling horns, fanny pack, etc. Small, rubber-coated hardware hooks that you can buy at Ace or Wal-Mart also work great for hanging and organizing your gear in a tree. The smaller hooks are easier to screw into a hardwood tree.

Backpack straps: Attach padded backpack straps to all your fixed-position and climbing stands (most new perches come with straps). Packing a stand on your back is the quietest and most comfortable way to get it into and out of the woods.

Limb saw: You'll need a small, folding saw to trim low-lying limbs before working a climber up a tree. Use a saw to carve out spots for a fixed-position or ladder stand, and for trimming shooting lanes.

Hand clippers: A pair of pruning shears comes in handy for trimming faint trails into your stand sites. Use a clipper to trim away small branches, vines and brush as you hang a stand. Once in a perch and ready to hunt, reach out and clip limbs or leaves that obscure your sight line or catch the tip of your bow or gun.

Pull-up rope: Use a 20-foot nylon rope to hoist up a 20-pound fixed-position stand. Once your stand is hung, use the cord to pull up your bow, unloaded firearm, fanny pack and other gear.

Bow holder: Consider bolting a small bow holder to the base of your fixed or climbing stand. It will hold your compound vertically and inches out of reach, freeing your hands for glassing, rattling, etc. You can also hang your bow on a screw-in step.

Always rope up an unloaded gun with action open and muzzle down.

Cables & locks: For around $15, you can install a tree-stand security system, which is good insurance on a heavily hunted public or private area. Use the rubber-coated cables and locks to secure a high-dollar ladder or climbing stand to a tree.

Observatory Stands

I hang dozens of tree stands in various corners of my hunting areas each fall. Many of them are not for hunting, but for mere observation.

Observatory stands work best anywhere the habitat is a quilt of crop fields, pastures and woodlots woven together with linear creek bottoms, fencerows and strips of woods. Hang a perch on a ridge, hillside or similar vantage where you can see 100 yards or farther. If the season is open, climb up with your bow or rifle. If a good buck happens to walk by, take him; but you're mostly there to glass the dawn and dusk hours with an 8x or 10x binocular, looking for bucks skulking along edges, around points and through thickets, funnels and creek crossings.

Hang an observatory stand and glass for a buck working a distant ridge or draw. Once you figure out his pattern, move in and set up for the kill.

The more times you spot a big deer exhibiting a similar movement pattern, the better off you are. Then one day when the wind is right, you can sneak in tighter to his core area and hang a hunting stand for a quick-strike ambush. The best part about the strategy is that it's low impact. When you study deer from an observatory stand on the fringes, a mature buck never knows you're there. He never sees, hears or smells you in his core area, which makes him a little easier to hunt when you finally move in and try to close the deal.

Modern Gear Tip: The days of the safety belt or even the chest harness are gone. Every tree stand hunter should now wear a full-body harness, which features not only midsection and shoulder straps, but also adjustable leg straps that cinch to your thighs and snug up against your butt. Recent studies by the Occupational Safety and Health Administration and others show that a full-body harness provides maximum protection and safety. In the event of a fall, a harness would spread the shock load over your body and keep you upright and in control. You should have enough time to recover from a slip before serious injury occurs, and you might be able to climb back onto a stand or yell to someone nearby for help. Simply put, a full-body harness might save your life. Several tree-stand manufacturers offer full-body harnesses designed specifically for whitetail hunting. Buy one and never hunt without it.

Hanging Tricks

Use these three tricks to fine-tune your stand placement and see more deer, regardless of where or when you hunt.

Play an obstacle. Say you find a huge fallen tree in a draw ... or a sinkhole on a ridge ... or a steep rock face on a hillside. Deer cannot or will not walk through, over or across such an obstacle; they'll skirt it every time. Play off that. Often you'll find a well-traveled trail around one side of an obstacle. Hang a tree stand downwind of the natural funnel.

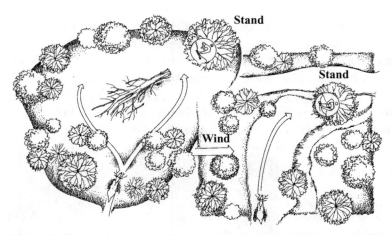

Figure 9. *Playing an obstacle when placing your stands can lead to a full freezer.*

Corner a buck. Position a stand in the downwind side of any sharp turn in the terrain such as the corner of a fence in the woods or a bend in a ridge or creek. An "inner corner" can squeeze deer within shooting range of your perch.

Get wet. Well, not literally. But you can never go wrong hanging a stand near a narrow creek crossing, slough edge, or river ford pocked with lots of fresh tracks.

Chapter 8

Strike Early

As mentioned in Chapter 2, you ought to start your pre-season scouting in July or early August. On hazy, sultry evenings, glass for bucks that come to graze and strut their stuff for does in crop fields, power-line cuts, new cutovers and other openings in your hunt zone. If you're like most of today's hunters, however, you're busy with your job, your kids, chores around home and all sorts of other stuff. In late summer chances are you're probably only thinking about scouting.

When bucks are still locked into a summer bed-to-feed pattern, you can set up on a trail near feed and whack a whopper like this.

Well, stop your procrastinating!

If you live in, or travel to, one of the 20-some states where the season opens in August or

September, you can make your scouting sessions a whole lot more fun and interesting by actually hunting the whitetails. Understand one thing, though. In late August or September, bucks are a different breed than you might be used to hunting.

From a behavioral perspective, deer, which haven't been hassled by hunters for 8 months or so, are more docile (read less spooky) than they'll be later in the season. Also, in late summer, does and bucks are much more predictable in their travels (read easier to pattern) than they will be come the wild days of the rut. When whitetails are locked into a bed-to-feed pattern, I find that things like a full moon and/or warm weather don't affect their daily movements nearly as much as they do later in the fall and winter.

A cool thing about hunting early is you never know what kinds of racks you'll see. A few bucks wear antlers still encased in velvet; others have racks adorned with peeling, bloody vascular skin. Many big deer have freshly polished, shining beams and tines. It adds an element of intrigue to the pursuit.

Field Games

When I started archery hunting whitetails out West in the early, early season, I did what came naturally. I'd glass big-racked bucks in the alfalfa fields down by the rivers, get all fired up, and rush in to hang tree stands on the edges of the food sources. Nothing to it, right?

In late September or early October, scout for fresh tracks on field edges and beneath mast trees.

Wrong. I learned the hard way that you can't just set up on edges that look good, and where you spotted deer the evening before.

A lot of the time my stands were only 40 to 50 yards off target, but that might as well be a mile when you're archery hunting. I saw a lot of big deer, but they were just out of shooting range.

If you go about it right, the hunting of white-tailed deer is a continual learning curve. I soon figured out that even when the season opens in September, it often pays to sacrifice a couple more evenings of hunting for scouting. That is tough for most people to do, but believe me, it is the smart thing to do. Come to think of it, the experienced guys who scout more than they actually hunt anywhere and anytime of the season are the ones who shoot big deer consistently.

Set up well off a feeding area and, with a good binocular and/or spotting scope, study deer movements. Spend extra time finding the *exact* trails or funnels bucks are walking out of the surrounding timber and brush. Then move in one day when the wind is right, hang a stand quietly on a crop edge and surprise a big deer in just the right spot. Having fine-tuned my strategy like that, I've gone from ogling and spooking a bunch of big deer to shooting Pope & Young bruisers inside 20 yards.

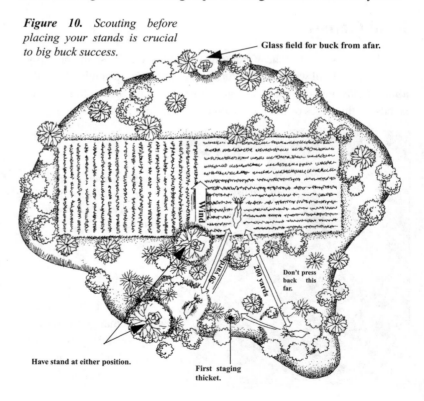

Figure 10. *Scouting before placing your stands is crucial to big buck success.*

Glass field for buck from afar.

Wind

50 yards

200 yards

Don't press back this far.

Have stand at either position.

First staging thicket.

"One of my favorite rut tactics is to still-hunt with a climber on my back, looking for heavy chasing action," says Darrell Daigre of West Point, Miss. "If I spot a good buck with a doe, I sneak into the area and climb. In the heat of the rut, deer might not pay much attention to your movements, noise or even your scent. More times than not, I end up in the thick of things. Sometimes I even spot several bucks with one hot doe."

"We key on four things: High-pressure, a rising barometer, cold temperatures and a rising moon in the evening or a falling moon in the morning," says Mark Drury of St. Peters, Mo. "On days when all those things line up, we often see 4 ½-year-old bucks moving hard."

"A big deer checks his scrapes at night," says Harold Knight of Cadiz, Ky. *"Just before sunrise, he beds down for a few hours. But along about 9 a.m. he often gets back up and starts prowling again. You might spot him right on up until lunchtime. The scrapes I watch are in thick cover back in the woods."*

"Four- to 6-year-old bucks lock antlers and try to kill each other," says Gary Roberson of Menard, Texas, one of the top rattlers in the country. *"There's awesome pushing and shoving, with dirt flying everywhere."* While the battles can be vicious, they are usually short-lived. *"Most bucks fight for 30 seconds or less,"* notes Roberson. *"That's why I rattle in short, hard bursts."*

Once you spot a Pope and Young buck, "don't just sit there and look at his rack," says Chuck Jones of Cadiz, Ky. "Watch the deer and anticipate his approach to your tree stand. Look 10 to 20 yards in front of the buck for shooting holes in the cover. Plan the shot in advance."

"I take all the big rubs and scrapes in an area into consideration," says David Hale of Cadiz, Ky. "Then I scout for a draw, point or creek crossing nearby. Downwind of a small funnel is usually where I hang a stand and hunt a buck putting down a lot of sign."

"During peak rut, an estrous doe can hold a mature buck in an area for two or three days," says Terry Drury of Bloomsdale, Mo. "As the buck tends the doe in a thicket, you might not see him. But hang in there in your best stand. When the big deer is finished with the doe, he'll go on the prowl again, and now you might see him."

One of my top rut tactics is to hang a rifle stand on a ridge where I can cover two or more draws or creek drainages. I expect to see deer chasing down in the funnels, and often I do. But I also keep an eye on thickets around and behind me. One day I was glassing a doe in a funnel when this beautiful 8-pointer popped out of a ridge thicket and walked into my lap.

Only a stud with a big rack and a swollen neck can thrash and gouge a tree like this. A "violent rub" is not only the sign of a good buck, but also an aggressive buck. A brazen deer will prowl far and wide for does, which gives you a fighting chance of seeing him in daylight hours.

Saskatchewan is my favorite place to hunt big deer. To me, nothing compares with the sight of a muscle-rippling, 300-pound, gnarly-racked buck ghosting though the Canadian bush. Mossy Oak producer/cameraman Troy Ruiz and I shot this great buck for a segment on the "American Hunter" TV show in November 2002.

The grunt call is one of the best innovations to come along in years. Never hunt without one! If you spot a buck walking over a ridge or ducking into cover, grunt loudly at him. Nine times out of 10 the deer will stop. With a gun, that might be the break you need. If you're archery hunting, keep grunting. The buck might turn in your direction.

You can't shoot a buck you can't see. I rely heavily on my Leica binoculars. I pick apart the woods or plains for a glinting tine, a patch of shiny hide or a flickering ear or tail. Once you find a piece of a deer, it's amazing how a whole buck pops into focus.

Staying mobile and flexible is a big key to hunting mature bucks these days. I like to pack a tree stand on my back and move in for a "quick-strike" ambush near a hot food source or in a funnel blazed with big rubs and scrapes.

If you hunt a small farm or woodland, you're best off in a tree stand most days. Your scent and silhouette are above deer. You don't walk around, spook bucks and push them off your property.

Small farms with a mix of crop fields and woodlands are producing mega bucks these days, like this awesome 165-incher. Try to lease a farm and implement a management program that revolves around three simple things: planting food strips or plots; shooting plenty of does; and letting 1 ½- and 2 ½-year-old bucks walk. You and your buddies and kids will have great hunting for years to come.

When a full moon overlaps the peak of the rut, deer move hard at night and again at midday. From Canada to Alabama to Texas, I've shot a bunch of good bucks trolling for does or flat-out chasing them between 10 a.m. and 2:30 p.m.

Eastern Lessons

I can hear some of you saying, "Sure, out West the country's big and the archery pressure is light. That's the reason whitetails are so easy to pattern. But what's the deal in a hard-core bowhunting state like Wisconsin, Minnesota, New York or Georgia?"

Point well taken. When tens of thousands of archers hit the woods in September, there's no denying the invasion has an impact on deer movements. Bucks still hit fields of clover, corn, soybeans, alfalfa and the like, but they begin to use multiple trails into and out of the feed. Too, deer become increasingly nocturnal around feeding areas as the season progresses and the pressure heats up. The bottom line is that you usually can't set your watch by the comings and goings of a good buck like you might out in Montana or Wyoming.

Still, you can make the most of the situation. Play the wind and hang a tree stand on the edge of a crop field, or better yet, on a nearby ridge or knoll with a commanding view of a feeding area. As discussed in Chapter 7, the "observatory" plan works great because it is low impact. If a good buck walks by your post some evening, thank your luck, draw and take him. But don't count on that happening. Your goal is to study the deer that show up at a food source at dusk.

Let's say you glass a gnarly 10-pointer stepping out of a creek bottom two evenings in a row. The third day, you hustle over there and find a spot for your stand. The next two nights, the big deer pops out into the field with some does 100 yards back toward your first setup. Reposition again, and again and again... Keep playing the wind and the cat and mouse game until you finally (hopefully) get a shot. Patience is usually rewarded in the early game.

Stage Time

Poof! Ever noticed how big bucks seem to vanish from fields come late September or early October? Well, the first thing you need to remember is that most of them don't go anywhere. Mature deer simply begin spending more time in the surrounding woods and thickets, where they gorge on falling acorns and fruits and hook trees with their antlers as they put on their game faces for the impending rut. Eventually the bucks might show up in the fields that you hunted earlier to feed and showboat for does, but it is often right at last shooting light or after dark;

Hunting in a thicket downwind of an oak flat is a great way to score big and early.

which means that in order to have a reasonable chance of sticking a big deer, you might have to hunt where he stages. It's risky business, but hey, why not go for it? Aggressive hunters are often the ones who bring home the heavy racks these days.

Here's the skinny on hunting stage left or stage right, whatever the case may be. One day around lunchtime put the wind in your face, or at least be sure it quarters back over your shoulder, and follow a main doe trail back into the cover that rims a field. Don't walk on the trail, but parallel it. Regardless of the terrain or cover, do not—I repeat, DO NOT—penetrate more than 100 to 200 yards. If you push any deeper than that into the cover, you're apt to jump bedded deer, and quite possibly the big buck you're trying to hunt. Bust him once and you make him jittery. Bust him twice and your gig is probably up.

Besides, at some point 100 yards or so off the field, the doe trail should splinter into two or three feeder paths. Whitetails typically come from all directions from back in the woods before funneling into the field along one or two main trails. Scout around for a trail junction emblazoned with two or three or more large, shredded rubs. You might also find some freshly pawed dirt, the first faux scrapes of fall, near a doe trail. In any event, check the wind—it must blow out of the cover and quarter somewhere back toward the field—and quietly hang a tree stand right there. You might nail a good buck prowling the trail intersection in the last glimmer of shooting light.

To make the strategy even better, look for acorns, as well as honey locust pods, persimmons, crab apples or other soft mast falling in a staging area. Check for lots of fresh deer tracks and droppings beneath the mast trees. Look for more rubs and pawings. If a bachelor group of bucks is staging in the vicinity, you're apt to find a mother lode of sign. Hang a stand there, or along one of those nearby feeder trails we just talked about.

Morning Hunts

Some of the best bowhunters I know sleep in. They figure that since the early-season hunting is so darn good in the evenings, why press bucks and possibly knock them off their patterns by hunting in the mornings? There is some merit to this, but let's get real. In these hectic times, you hunt when you can. If that happens to be a week of mornings in September or early October, you ought to go for it. Here are a couple of good strategies to try.

Sometimes does and a few bucks in the 120- to 140-class linger in and around fields and mast-rich staging areas at first light. You can hunt those deer if you can get in there without the animals seeing or smelling you, which is admittedly tricky.

Glass a field two or three mornings in a row, and focus on spots where deer linger and then filter back into the surrounding cover. Then check an aerial photo for a hidden route into one of your evening stands, or into a spot where you can hang a fresh morning perch and ambush a buck. The biggest challenge is getting to a hunting spot without busting deer heading back to their beds. Go extra early, a couple of hours before daybreak, and hope for the best. You might bump a few deer, but you might still get a crack at a straggler buck that comes by 30 minutes or an hour after sunup.

A couple of years ago out in eastern Montana, I was down to my last hunting day. My buddy decided to sleep in and hope for the best that afternoon. I was thinking differently and out of the box.

At 4 A.M. I climbed into a canoe and paddled by feel 100 yards down the Milk River. I beached the boat as quietly as I could, waded 50 yards, climbed a steep bank and snuck into a stand where I had spotted several good bucks the afternoon before. So far, so good. I hadn't heard any deer crashing away or blowing, so maybe I would get lucky. I climbed up and waited.

The sun rose and eight does tiptoed past before I saw a rack glittering in the muted light. He was no monster, but he was a great bow buck for the last day of a hunt 2000 miles from home. Moving back to his bed, the 125-class 8-pointer walked within nine steps of my tree. I launched a 2213 arrow with a Satellite broadhead and watched the double-lunged buck fall 60 yards away. I gutted him, dragged him back to the canoe, paddled back to camp, woke up my buddies and hollered, "Look what I got!"

When it's hot, you might shoot a buck on a thick ridge near a cool, shady stream or river.

My friend Brad Farris, a former guide who now works for Primos Hunting Calls and bowhunts mature whitetails across the country, put me onto an awesome morning tactic a few years ago. "Go in there and look for a little thicket on a ridge or point near the river," Farris told me as we prepped to hunt a property down in Mississippi. "It should be cool and breezy around the water, and there should be lots of green browse in there. When the weather is warm, and it usually is early in the season, deer love spots like that. If you can circle around a nearby field, sneak through the woods and slip tight to a bedding area along a river, creek or slough, you've got a good place for a morning stand."

If the opportunity presents itself, try to stick a good buck there some morning in September or early October. And of course keep trying to score on those prime evening hunts around a food source or in a staging area. It will be a great feeling if you do. There's nothing like early success to take the pressure off the rest of your whitetail season.

Quick Tip: A rub line that links a buck's bedding area and food source is a great clue, but it can be tough to find early in the season when the ground foliage is thick and the leaves are still on the trees. Scout for clusters of big rubs first. They're easiest to find. Then look out from those signposts for smaller rubs that give away a buck's travel route. If you still can't find a rub line, and in many areas you won't be able to, don't worry about it. Just hang your bow stand along a thick edge or near a draw, ditch or similar funnel where a big deer is likely to prowl.

Modern Gear Tip: Some magazine writers advise you to stick with a 100- or 125-grain, fixed-blade broadhead because it is rugged, dependable and offers good penetration. Other writers, or maybe a talking head on TV or a video, will say switch to a mechanical head because it is accurate and opens a big wound channel in a deer. Don't be swayed either way! Only you can decide which hunting head is best for you. Over the summer practice season, test a variety of fixed-blade and mechanical heads, and hunt with the one that flies the best out of your bow. Every time you shoot a doe or a buck, closely examine the broadhead's performance. If it flies true, hits hard and drops deer within 100 yards, stick with it. But if you're not all that impressed, don't be afraid to switch. Keep testing, tuning and looking for the broadhead—fixed-blade or open-on-impact—in which you have the most confidence. You'll hunt better for it.

Bow-Stand Savvy

Many hunters pack in a tree stand and fling it up into the first big tree that looks good. Not me. After 20 minutes or so of speed scouting

an area, I beat feet out of the woods, go home or back to camp and study my maps and aerials. I evaluate the terrain, food, cover and sign I just found. I piece things together and predict deer movements as best I can.

I don't hunt from skyscraper stands. Depending on the roll of the terrain and the cover in the trees, I feel most comfortable shooting a bow at 16 to 20 feet.

A few days before a hunt, I sneak back into an area a second time and set a stand for afternoon or morning hunting. I go at midday when the wind is right. I head for a spot where I have deduced that my chances of an ambush are high. I check to make sure deer are still running the same trails into or out of a field, and I monitor the status of the mast in a staging spot. I note any rubs or huge tracks that popped up since I was last there.

Then I look around for a stout tree downwind of an edge, trail or funnel. I back up 20 to 30 yards, kneel and check the treetop from a deer's perspective. If it offers adequate background cover, bingo!

I face most of my bow stands toward a crop field or a ridge or flat with hot mast. In the afternoons, most deer come from the woods and thickets to the rear, and the tree between you and them will provide great cover. If you shoot right-handed, try to set up where deer will pass within 30 yards to your left (vice versa for lefties). That way, you can draw and shoot with ease and little movement as a buck quarters past.

You might like to hunt 18 to 20 feet up a tree, but sometimes you can't do that in a late-summer or early-autumn jungle. If you sit too high, leafy limbs and thick ground foliage can make it difficult to see a buck, much less shoot him. Don't be afraid to set your perches 4 or 5 feet lower than normal. You'll still have good cover amid all the leaves, and you'll be able to see deer better. For scent-control reasons, I wouldn't hunt much below 15 feet.

Most of the time, you'll have to cut a few shooting lanes. Go for it, because it makes no sense to hunt from a stand that you can't shoot out of! Just don't get carried away and do a pulpwood job along a trail or in a staging area. Drag cut saplings and limbs downwind of your stand, where deer won't see or smell them. After hanging a stand and trimming, it is always a good idea to let a spot settle down for a day or two before hunting it.

When you come back, remember this mantra: *Access an evening stand from the food-source side, and make sure the wind quarters out of the woods.* Climb into your perch by 2 P.M. or so, especially if you hunt in the Midwest or West, where whitetails tend to get up and move earlier than in the East and South.

Okay, you're on stand and hunting. The afternoon fades. Some does tip past, but you haven't spotted antlers yet. Don't get down, get ready! As dusk settles into the woods, stand up, hold your bow and rest its lower wheel in a belt holster. A big deer often comes late and quickly to a crop field or mast tree, especially on a warm day. Listen for the *pop, pop, pop* of his hooves behind you.

A buck ghosting past your stand in the twilight often looks farther away than he really is. Don't risk taking too long of a shot, but on the other hand, don't let a shooter slip by at 25 or 30 yards. If in doubt, do a juggling act and try to laser a deer with your rangefinder. You ought to have lasered several shooting markers earlier in the afternoon.

Figure 11. *A right-handed shooter facing east wants a buck to show up in one of the three gray areas. Try to position your stand accordingly.*

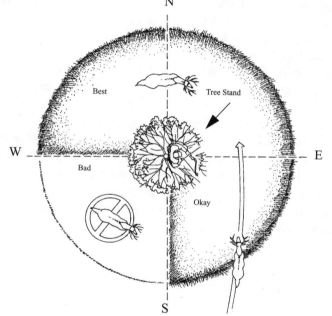

You've probably seen photographs of bowhunters standing on the front edge of tree stands, leaning way out and drawing down on deer. That makes for good photos, but I don't recommend it. Instead, sit or stand with your feet planted toward the back of the stand. Dig your back into the tree. Hold your bow vertically and close to your body, with an arrow nocked, of course. You'll be safe and well hidden. Keep that posture until a buck cruises within 25 yards. Then step or lean out, bend at the waist and shoot without getting busted.

When a buck is broadside, tuck a sight pin behind his front leg and on the lower third of his side. If he ducks when the string twangs, your arrow should still strike the middle or top of his lungs. If the deer doesn't drop you'll make an even better shot, low in the lungs and heart. When a buck quarters slightly away, remember to move your sight pin slightly back on his ribs. Broadside or quartering-away are the ONLY shots you should take.

If you double-lung a buck and see him fall, go get him. But when a deer bolts into thick foliage and you're not so sure about the shot, wait a couple of hours before tracking. Come back with a buddy and big, powerful lights.

Early in the season, a buck might wheel and run back toward a bedding area on a doe trail after being hit, so check there for blood. It's no wives' tale that an arrowed deer often runs downhill and toward water. I recently shot a buck and found him drifting in a creek at the foot of a draw a quarter-mile from my stand.

On all those evenings when shooting light wanes and you're left with a full quiver, sit awhile and glass deer that still cruise toward a field or mill around mast. Who knows, you might spot a whopper buck you've never seen before, and you can come back and hunt him another day. When the deer move on and the coast is clear, slip out of your stand. By now you should have mapped out an exit route that will take you 50 yards or so back into the woods and away from the feeding area. Circle back to your truck without spooking deer and guess what? Your chances of sticking a buck are good to excellent when you come back and hunt the next afternoon or the one after that.

Chapter 9

Super Rut Sets

I peered down the ridge and shivered. *Whoa, he's thick as an Angus*, I thought. The buck marched toward my stand in a stiff-legged gait, his nose working the ground like a Hoover, his rack glinting in the morning sunshine. I eased up my 50-caliber muzzleloader and fired. The smoke cleared, and I watched the heavy 10-pointer topple over 75 yards away. I pumped my fist and hollered, "Awesome!"

You might see a giant 10-pointer like this once all season—one morning during peak rut. Shoot straight and seize the day!

The early and late seasons are the best times to pattern mature bucks and hunt them on their natural movement patterns. But on the fun meter, nothing comes close to hunting the rut. For a couple of wild weeks in the fall or winter, bucks throw caution to the wind and lollygag around the woods, sniffing for the intoxicating aroma of *eau de doe*. Other studs are beyond that. They're on the lam, chasing the girls or having their way with them in thickets.

The truth is, you never know what you might see each day. Some does but nary a buck ... a couple of spindly racked 6-pointers running around like testosterone-addled teenagers ... or a 160-inch deer hot after a doe. Of course the latter is what you want. Try to make it happen from one of these rut sets.

The Rub Cluster

During the middle and latter stages of the pre-rut, scout like a madman for a cluster of rubs in an out-of-the-way thicket. You might find some of the fall's first scrapes nearby. A big deer often thrashes 10, 20 or more trees (some big, some small) in a spot to vent sexual frustration and advertise his presence to does and other bucks.

Position a tree stand downwind of a rubbed pocket where a buck is hanging out and priming for the breeding season. You are not hunting over the rubs per se, but you are sure watching for the buck in a thick corner of his home core area. Being early in the rut, the deer probably won't move much at midday, but you might catch him on his hooves at dawn or dusk. Watch close.

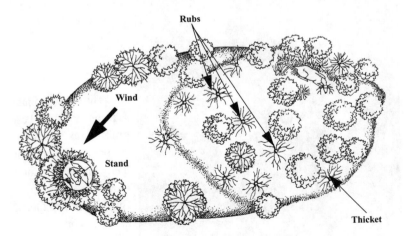

Figure 12. During the pre-rut it may be easier to find rub clusters than individual rubs.

The Cover Scrape

Scrapes, the most alluring of all buck sign, have had hunters chasing their tails for years. Ongoing research, while interesting, hasn't helped much, and in many cases has only added to the confusion. For example, some scientists suggest that some young bucks paw several hundred scrapes only to abandon half, three-quarters or even all of them. Other studies show that old, dominant bucks scrape sporadically, but they work lick branches year-round. I read the other day that some does scrape!

The scientific community is equally split on why whitetails scrape. The conventional thinking is that a buck paws an oval and urinates over his hocks into the bare soil; he then licks and rubs his forehead, nostrils and eyes on an overhead branch to attract does to the area and to indicate his burning desire to breed them. But now some biologists speculate that male dominance might have more to do with the ritual. They say bucks with overlapping home ranges make and check scrapes to keep tabs on one another. Still other experts say bucks probably scrape to satisfy both of the aforementioned functions.

Baffled? Me too. But from a hunting perspective, you just need to remember two things. First, deer use scrapes as some means of olfactory communication, as complex and uncertain as it is. Second, to strike pay dirt and kill a big buck, you simply need to hunt the right scraped area at the right time. You should start off by hunting a "cover scrape."

In addition to being a highly nocturnal devil, a mature 8- or 10-pointer is a cover-hugger. A buck spends a lot of time on wooded ridges and in draws and creek bottoms laced with brush, green browse and the like, and that is where you'll find a lot of rubs and scrapes. The more secluded the scrapes, the better, I think. Hang a stand or set a blind nearby and you've got a decent shot of catching a good buck milling around them in shooting light.

Trail Rubs & Scrapes

A mature buck begins prowling around to take the estrus temperature of does in late October in most states, and a month or two later in some regions of the Deep South. But rather than cruising down a main doe trail like he might have done when he was locked in on feed earlier

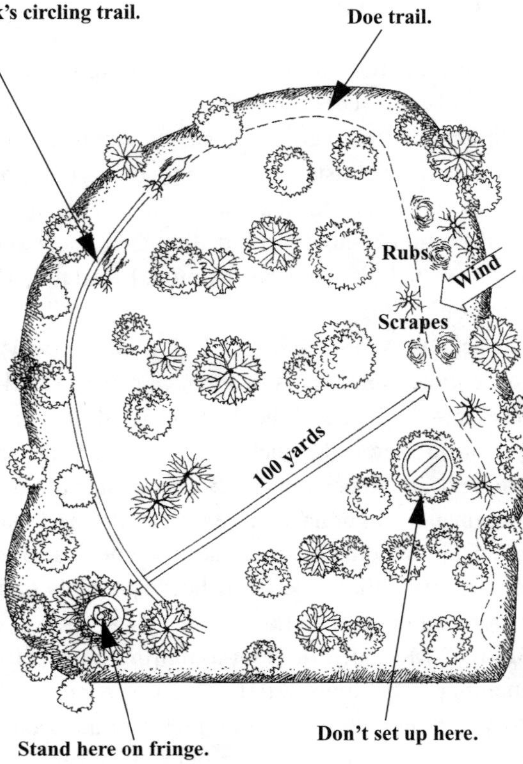

Buck's circling trail.

Doe trail.

Figure 13. Bucks like to circle downwind of doe trail scrapes. If setup is too close to sign, they might see or smell you. Back off 100 yards or so.

Rubs

Wind

Scrapes

100 yards

Stand here on fringe.

Don't set up here.

in the season, now a buck is apt to cut through thickets and skirt a doe run on the downwind side. Occasionally, though, he'll mosey up to sniff the trail proper, and that is where you'll find some smoking rubs and scrapes.

Check out the scrapes, but really examine those rubs. A young 6-pointer might scrape like crazy in a doe run, but he can rub a sapling only so big and so violently. On the other hand, a dominant 10-pointer might paw only a so-so scrape, but he might get mad and thrash a tree as thick as your calf. Big rubs near hot scrapes—that's the sign you should look for.

On an evening hunt, set up in a thicket downwind of a scraped-and-rubbed doe trail that winds toward a crop field, food plot or ridge with falling acorns. At dawn, play the wind and watch a sign-blazed trail near a doe-bedding area deep in the woods.

Big rubs near scrapes on a ridge or in a draw—that's the sign to look for.

"Mini" Scrape Lines

As mentioned many times in this book, whitetail patterns have changed, and are forever changing, in the broken farmlands and woodlands that most of us hunt today. Deer densities are high in many small, diverse habitats. Bucks might have to travel only a mile or so to find feed, cover, water and plenty of does during the rut. To wit, most bucks don't lay down long, meandering scrape lines like their ancestors did 10 or 20 years ago.

But bucks are bucks. When the testosterone begins to roil big time, they rub and paw as they move short distances from their beds to feed and back again. Check for their "mini" scrape lines in strips of timber, along brushy fencerows, in draws between ridges and fields, on the edges of sloughs … you get the idea.

Many of today's short scrape lines are heavily tended because so many deer walk past them so frequently. Trouble is, mature bucks with tight patterns move and scrape mostly at night, even in the frat-party atmosphere of the late pre-rut, which means that most of the time they'll be curled in their beds when you watch their sign.

One solution to this dilemma is to scout for a mini scrape line that wends toward a marsh, overgrown field, ridge thicket or similar cover where you suspect a mature buck lies up. Try to set up where a deer's scrapes peter out just before his bedding site. You might catch a glimpse of the big guy because those last scrapes are the first ones he sniffs as he prowls forth at dusk, and they are the last ones he checks as he sneaks back to cover at dawn.

Community Scrapes

On a turkey hunt one April I ran across a huge scrape a mile deep in a woodlot. It was old and dry, but it showed a couple of fresh hoof prints and rake marks. Most intriguing was the overhead lick branch that had been twisted and snapped the previous fall. Looking close, I noticed that the limb had been recently chewed and worked by deer. I really didn't know what to make of things, but I went home and marked the location of that scrape on an aerial photograph.

A community scrape sits in a high-interaction area where lots of does and bucks travel and mingle year-round.

One day the following November I scouted the spot and found that old scrape was now the size of a truck hood! It was black and reeked of tarsal. I hung a stand downwind of it, and over the course of 3 days, I saw 30 deer, including eight racked bucks, prowling through the area. I killed the best one, a heavy 9-pointer, with my bow.

There is nothing mysterious about a community scrape. It simply sits in a high-interaction area where lots of does and bucks travel year-round. Best of all from a hunting perspective, all sorts of deer mingle in the area during the breeding season.

The bowhunter has a couple of options. You can either set up within shooting range of a big scrape, or you can hang back 100 yards or so downwind. Deer cruise into and around a big scrape from all directions and many bucks angle in from the downwind side. So, like most scrape-hunting decisions, it's really a crapshoot.

I generally opt for the latter option and hang a bow stand well off a scrape, in thick cover and somewhere downwind. This lessens the chances of deer seeing or smelling me as I sneak in, and I have a good, wide view of the breeding commune as I hunt. I try to set up near a doe trail, or at least within arrow range of a thick edge where a buck might walk. I always hang a muzzleloader or rifle stand 100 yards or farther off a community scrape, high in a tree where I can see well all around.

It is important to remember that your goal is not to kill a buck working a scrape, or poking his nose into one. That happens, but it's rare. Just play the wind and set up near a community scrape or scrape line in a thick, remote spot. You might hit pay dirt.

The Ridge Perch

I find that across the country and especially in the South, bucks like to troll for does along ridges laced with green thickets, second-growth saplings, thinned pines or the like. Scout a ridge for a main doe trail that is worn to the ground with fresh tracks and hook a tree stand downwind of it. Again, it's hard to tell what you'll see. A good buck might lollygag down the trail, nose to the ground. Or he might parallel the path, skulking through cover on the downwind side. Or he might pop out of a thicket and cut the trail at a choke point. Keep on edge and keep rolling your eyes in all directions.

As mentioned previously in this book, most days the wind and thermals are fairly steady and predictable on a ridge or hillside. That's good for a buck as he tries to sniff out a doe. It's great for you as you set up and try to cut short his heated mission. Hunt on the high side of a ridge trail whenever you can.

Stay on Edge

Pines meet hardwoods, cedars border oak brush, honeysuckle rims a cutover or burn … Bucks are notorious for traveling edges, where they often rub and scrape along the way. Try hanging a bow stand in a dark, dense edge where big deer like to travel. When hunting with a scoped rifle or slug gun, set up 75 to 100 yards away and watch a long edge, or better yet, two or three fringes that come together.

A great place to shoot a buck is in "broken" country dotted and laced with woods, thickets and fields. Watch for deer scraping and traveling the many edges.

The Ridge/Creek Setup

Let's see, there was a gnarly 9-pointer in Virginia, a good 8 in Missouri and a tall-tined 10 in Mississippi. I shot those bucks one season from tree stands set where two or more ridges petered out into creek bottoms. Anytime you can hunt this type of setup, do it. The bases of ridges and the edges of creeks (or rivers, sloughs or oxbow lakes) are often rimmed with tight cover and pocked with deer tracks, rubs and scrapes. In many instances, the terrains form 3- or 4-sided funnels that squeeze does and bucks within bow or gun range.

The Watering Hole

Sometimes I hang out at a local watering hole during the rut. Not Pete's Grill or Molly's Irish Pub, but a secluded pond, slough or creek pool rimmed with thick brush. When deer run and chase, they get thirsty. Several does and a wild-eyed buck are liable to show up at a waterhole anytime of day.

Hunting near water is an obvious tactic for one of the hot, dry ruts we are accustomed to these days, but try it during cold weather as well.

If all the waterholes in your area are frozen tight, bust a hole in a pond or pool and hang a tree stand nearby. The offbeat tactic works best in a dry, arid region, or anywhere creeks or waterholes are few and far between.

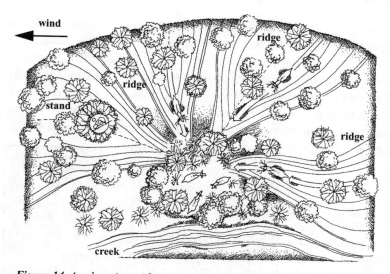

Figure 14. *Any location with two or more ridges petering out in a creek bottom deserves a second look.*

The Overgrown Field

In Alabama one December, I sat in a stand and watched eight porcelain tines weave through a maze of grass, honeysuckle and newly planted pines. As I raised my rifle to scope the buck's shoulder, the rack disappeared. The deer bedded down before my eyes.

I wasn't surprised. A field or cutover with cover head high to a buck is a prime bedding ground. After a long night of mingling with does, a big deer often sneaks out into a "dirty" spot and curls up with his back to the wind. If he smells, sees or hears danger, the buck slips away like a rabbit through the thick stuff.

Scout the edges of a large cover for trails, tracks, rubs and scrapes. Check for narrow, twisting trails gouged into the cover. Then play the wind and hang a tree stand strategically along the perimeter, where you can see and shoot out into the thick stuff. You might ambush a buck as he slips into the cover at daybreak, or skulks out to contact does in late afternoon. If you hang tough at midday, you might get a crack at a good deer when he stands up to stretch, browse or nose a nearby doe.

The Timber Strip

Here's a great setup for the Midwest, or anywhere a maze of linear covers connect crop fields, pastures and large and small woodlands.

Scan an aerial photograph for a strip of timber that is narrow enough to funnel deer, yet large enough to hold multiple stands or blinds that you can hunt on different winds. Most of the time a strip, especially if it is laced with mast trees and satellite thickets, is a high-interaction area for deer, and thus it is pocked with a mother lode of trails, tracks, rubs and scrapes.

A narrow strip of timber or a recently thinned pocket is a great spot to shoot a buck.

All whitetails, and especially mature bucks, like to cling to cover when traveling between major feeding and bedding areas. You might spot a shooter buck running a strip during any phase of the season, but my favorite time to hunt one is during the scraping phase and into the breeding time, when a big deer prowls mindlessly for the first estrous does. Hang a tree stand tight to a trail or buck sign when archery hunting. When gun hunting, back off 100 yards or so and try to cover two or three strips that bucks might use.

The Timber Funnel

One morning I climbed into a tree stand I had hung a week earlier in the head of a long oak hollow. When the sun rose I would have a good view of several rolling ridges and draws, as well as a brush-choked creek bottom 100 yards below. There wasn't a food source in sight, and the nearest bedding area was a mile away. It was a perfect spot for an ambush.

Four-wheelers whined on the next farm. The sun rose and 270s and '06s cracked all around. It was, after all, gun season and the peak of the rut. There's gonna be pressure and lots of it in most areas. Deal with it and factor it into your plan.

When the rut and gun season overlap, your strategy is simple: Hang a stand where you can cover multiple thickets, and watch for bucks pushing does in the covers or moving in there to flee the pressure.

The sun rose and an 8-pointer with thin tines and a gleam in his eye chased a doe down a ridge. The pair plunged into a honeysuckle thicket, and I figured the lad had gotten lucky and was breeding her in there, though I could not be sure. Anyway, I had to turn my attention to the sound of deer scrambling in the leaves. Somebody had scared the wits out of two bucks, which rumbled over a ridge and dove into a draw to my right. The lead deer was a pig, 200 pounds plus, and his rack was dark and heavy. I dropped him with a 130-grain bullet.

In early fall you need to locate multiple food sources and bedding areas, and methodically scout for trails, tracks, rubs and scrapes. But when the rut cranks and the gun hunters hit the woods, blowing up the patterns of deer, you can pretty much forget all that tedious stuff. It is now time to employ the simplest yet deadliest tactic of all. Set up in a funnel where you can see a long way, and watch for bucks sprinting after does or fleeing pressure.

Funnels come in all shapes and sizes: finger ridges; draws; ditches; the edges of swamps, sloughs or creek bottoms; strips of timber that link fields; long, grassy ravines out West ... to name just a few. Keep a few things in mind when deciding which corridor to hunt:

- Choose a draw or creek bottom in an area where you spotted a big deer a couple of times in October or early November. The buck should hang in his core area and prowl that funnel often during the rut.
- The thicker the cover in a funnel, the better.
- The more doe trails on a ridge and in adjacent draws, the better the odds that a buck will rut there. The "hunt the does" strategy certainly applies to funnels.
- Hunt a thick, secluded, hot-looking draw or slough edge, even if there's not a lot of buck sign there. Once guns have boomed for a few days or a week, deer will find the funnel and pile into it.
- Try to access a funnel from a ridge, and hang a tree stand on the upper side of it, where you can see down and across several ridges and draws. Also, from a high setup, you can glass down into thickets for bucks.

When the weather is cool and the rut is kicking, climb into your stand and sit tight for hours, or even all day if you have the fortitude. You'll see a lot of deer in a funnel, and sooner or later a good buck might gallop by.

In Alabama one January, I shot an old 8-pointer nosing a doe in a strip of dry ground bordered on all sides by sloughs—time, 2:30 p.m. The next day, a friend of mine dropped a 145-inch 10-pointer chasing four does through the same funnel—time, 9:20 a.m. During the main rut, good things can happen during the mid-morning and early-afternoon hours, so be out there.

Satellite Thickets

An old, rut-crazed buck might chase a doe round and round a crop field or pasture, but a lot of times I don't see it. I'm too busy hunting back in the timber, where I feel my odds of spotting a wall-hanger are better. Having been hassled by hunters for days or weeks in many areas, many old does forsake fields during daylight hours. They do, however, head for satellite covers 100 yards or so off feeding areas, where they browse and glean mast right up until the day they are ready to breed. Hang a tree stand downwind of a thicket and watch for a buck hassling the gals until he finds a hot one.

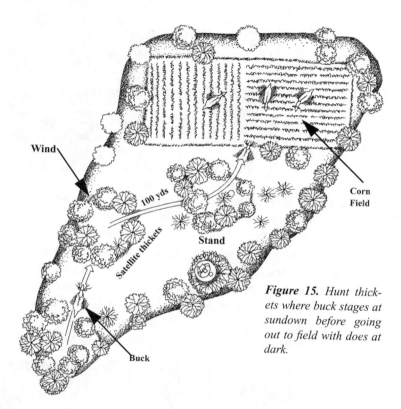

Figure 15. *Hunt thickets where buck stages at sundown before going out to field with does at dark.*

To this I need to add a disclaimer. Sometimes just days before the peak of the rut, does will actually avoid the thickets and move out into fields and other open areas. Not quite ready to breed, the gals don't want the bucks to hem them up in thick cover, so they move out into wide-open spaces, especially in late afternoon. In so doing, the gals pull some mighty good bucks out of hiding. If and when bucks are noticeably visible in fields, cutovers, power-line cuts and the like, by all means set up and hunt there.

Where'd They Go?

Say it's November 10th in Illinois, December 18th in Mississippi or January 20th in south Alabama. The weather is perfect, overcast and in the 30s, and the wind is calm. You're off work and pumped to hunt the peak.

A buck might hole up with an estrous doe for 1 to 3 days.

© *Charles J. Alsheimer*

You sit in a stand or blind all day and see a few does and spindly bucks, but neither hide nor hair of a big deer. You go back the next day and hunt your second best stand. Same thing. What gives?

Well, as luck would have it, you're probably hunting the peak-breeding phase in your neck of the woods. The big boys are holed up in thickets, cedars or pines and having their way with mature does. All you can do is keep hunting your best stands on ridges and near funnels and secluded thickets. In a day or two, once those first does are bred, the bruisers will start cruising again. Actually, the week following the initial breeding surge is one of my favorite times to hunt for a big deer back on the prowl for girls.

You never know what you might see in the rut. I photographed this doe rub-urinating in a scrape!

Rutting-Buck Body Language

- **Ears back:** A sex-crazed buck might march toward your stand with his ears pinned back and his hackles up. Shoot when you can. A dominant deer looking to kick some butt—maybe he hears or smells a rival male nearby—might stand in one spot and drool for 2 minutes. Or he might crash off in a split-second. Close the deal when and if you can.
- **Nose down:** A big deer that walks along with his nose working the ground like a vacuum cleaner is consumed with one thing: smelling and sorting out the scent of a hot doe. If you stay calm and quiet he might walk into shooting range, and perhaps ridiculously close. I've had sniffing bucks come within 5 yards of my tree stands and ground blinds, never knowing I was there.

A dominant buck postures his rack and bristles his hair to show a subordinate male who's the boss.

© Charles J. Alsheimer

- **Nose up:** A buck working the wind and "lip curling" is also trying to sort out doe scent. Be careful, especially if you're up in a tree stand. Since his nose and eyes are up and back, a buck might see you and spook if you draw your bow or move your rifle at the wrong time. Wait until a buck turns or drops his head before setting up the shot.
- **Hooves popping:** You might not be able to see a buck, but you can often hear his stiff-legged gait a long way off in dry leaves. Get ready because he's coming! The deer probably won't be with a doe, but he'll be prowling hard for one. If you spot the buck out of shooting range or walking the wrong way, rattle, grunt or bleat to get his attention. He's stoked to respond.

Stalk the Rut

Sneak 30 yards … lean against a tree … watch and listen for 10 minutes … slip another 20 yards. Man, I've smoked a bunch of rutting bucks that way with a muzzleloader and a rifle.

Often a buck will chase a doe round and round a 50 to 100-acre patch. Stalk in slow and tight downwind of the deer and you might get a shot.

Stalking the rut has several advantages. First, you cover a lot of ground, which increases your odds of bumping into a buck trolling for does or chasing one. Also, the more terrain you cover each day, the more smoking rubs, scrapes and big tracks you'll find. You can come back the next day, hang a stand and maybe get the buck that is putting down that sign.

Quick Tip: Say one morning you hear loud, deep-pitched gurgles in a nearby thicket. Man, get ready! Chances are a big buck has cornered a doe in there, and he's talking to her with what I call "gargling grunts" (biologists call them tending grunts). If the gal is not ready to stand and breed, she'll soon bust out of the cover with the crazed boy on her heels. Shoot quickly if you can.

Stay high on ridges and hillsides, but don't skyline. Use a wind-checking device and keep the breeze quartering across your face as you pad along. Move slowly, pause beside trees and watch for deer moving in funnels and bottoms. Use your nose. Rutting bucks pee over their hocks and reek of tarsal scent. You can smell 'em a long way off, like you can smell elk.

Modern Gear Tip: These days my passion is hunting the rut with a muzzleloader. Most of the time, I carry a 50-caliber Knight Magnum DISC rifle, topped with a 2x-7x Leupold Vari-X scope. With 250-grain saboted bullets pushed by 100 or 150 grains Pyrodex, I get 2-inch groups at 100 yards, and I feel comfortable shooting at a buck out to 150. Bolting a plastic disc with a 209 primer into the rifle's action, I have confidence the gun will go BOOM when I tip the trigger. Some days I use a Thompson/Center Encore 209x50 Magnum. The break-open hammer gun, which also uses the 209 ignition system, is well-balanced, reliable and accurate.

Stalking works best if you and a buddy have the sole hunting rights to a farm or woodlot. You can sneak around without the worry of bumping into strangers. Heck, if you bump a buck, you might nudge him past your pal's post.

Chapter 10

Pressure Plans

A motorcade of trucks and SUVs rolls through the countryside. Doors slam. ATVs fire up. Flashlights flicker. Human stink floods the woods as pumpkin-colored hunters race for their stands. It takes, oh, about a nanosecond for whitetails to remember the drill. I believe old does and bucks know the season has begun *before* the first rifle cracks at dawn.

Morning hunts are best during gun season. Some bucks move well on their own at first light, while others are pushed by people walking to their stands. Either way you might see and shoot a good one.

Moderate to heavy pressure, especially during gun season and the rut, is a fact of life in most areas these days. You'd better learn to deal with the heat and factor it into your annual hunting plan.

Hang Tough

Scouting a week before rifle season one November, a buddy and I spotted a couple of 10-pointers roaming our lease. Man, were we fired up! We figured those deer would score in the 150s. On opening weekend we passed on buck after buck, hoping for a crack at one of the big boys.

While we didn't shoot, wow, other guys sure did. *Crack, zing, whump.* For two days shots rang through the countryside, and you could hear bullets strike some deer. After, oh, about the 100th shot we began to wonder if any bucks could have possibly made it.

"Heck with it, I'm going back to the cornfield stand," John said on the third day. He sucked it up and hiked into the spot he'd hunted the previous evenings.

I heard his 270 bark at dusk. When I drove up a half-hour later, my truck's headlights illuminated my grinning buddy and his awesome 10-pointer— one of those 150-inchers!

You spend a lot of time scouting and hanging tree stands for a reason. Either you spot a good buck in an area before the season, or you find big rubs, scrapes and tracks in a spot. Well, once the guns start booming, don't get all flustered, start second-guessing yourself and give up on a stand too early. More mature bucks than you think survive the initial gauntlet of shots and cling to their patterns for a few days, especially if your gun season overlaps the rut, when bucks are goofy for does. Keep the faith; hang tough in your best stands and you still might score.

Long shots from a tree stand can be tough. Try to hang your perch so you have a solid rifle rest.

You should always keep legal shooting hours in mind when you hunt near a crop field or other feeding area because a mature buck will probably show up right at dark if he shows at all.

You can get lucky in the afternoon, but I think your chances are better when you hunt a morning stand back in the timber. When the heat is on, an old deer feels most comfortable cruising around or chasing a doe on a hardwood ridge or in a secluded draw or creek bottom. He knows that by now he should have gone completely nocturnal, but the woods give him a false sense of security. He thinks he's hidden in the trees, but he's not if you're posted back in there. Set up early and look for a buck ghosting around at the crack of dawn.

Watch "Tier Thickets"

In some areas, you can study an aerial map and see tiers of small and large thickets that wend back into the woods. It can make for some great hunting during the first week of the season. Most of your competition will park their trucks, walk to the first thicket 200 to 300 yards away and hunt right there. Outsmart those guys by circling around and hunting the next deeper thicket, one that you know from scouting holds big rubs, tracks and scrapes. Get there early and hang a tree stand or take a seat on a ridge or hillside where you can see a couple hundred yards. If

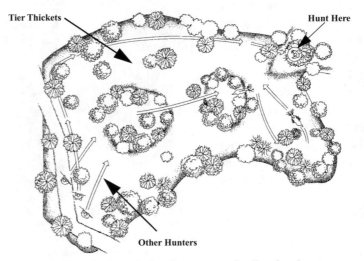

Figure 16. Hunting "tier thickets" can prove deadly when hunting pressure increases.

you can cover a couple of escape funnels and see beyond the second thicket and into the third one, that's better yet. Chances are other hunters will push deer out of thickets near roads and parking areas. You might get a buck sneaking into the deeper cover you are watching.

If you don't tag out early one morning, hang tough for the rest of the day. Actually, one of my favorite times to hunt anywhere in the country is from 10 A.M. until 2:30 P.M. Most other hunters have headed for home or camp, so there's less pressure in the woods. Whitetails seem to sense that, and they often rise from their beds to stretch and browse. If the rut is on, things can get interesting. A mature buck might get up and prowl. He'll likely skirt areas that received heavy pressure earlier that morning, but he might feel safe sniffing for estrous does around a tier of secluded thickets. That's where you're set up, and you might get a shot.

Around 2 P.M. you'll hear trucks roaring down country roads again. An ATV might whine a half-mile away. Keep your eyes glued on the edges of those thickets. As guys hit the woods for the afternoon hunt, they might drive a buck into your sights.

Find the "Buck Holes"

By day five of gun season your stands on the edges of fields and in

open timber will probably have gone cold. Now the surviving bucks are secretive night owls. You've got to find what I call "buck holes." These are tangles of honeysuckle or wild rose on ridges, cedar or pine thickets, overgrown fields, brushy beaver swamps, etc.

A small thicket or ditch overlooked by other hunters is a good spot to kill a buck late in the season.

Contrary to popular belief, a buck hole doesn't have to be large or even remote. If other hunters overlook it, a grassy ditch near a back road or maybe an overgrown hog lot behind a farmer's barn can hold a big buck. Sometimes it pays to think small.

Scour an aerial photograph for pockets or strips of cover off the beaten path, and then one morning play the wind and still-hunt slowly toward a buck hole. Who knows, you might get lucky and nail a big deer on the way in. If not, do some low-impact scouting. Check the edges of a thicket or swamp for trails pocked with big tracks. Check for fresh rubs and scrapes, sign that a buck has moved back in there to evade hunters and breed a few does.

If you find a big lode of hot sign, slam on the brakes and stop right there. You sure don't want to bust into a security area, put more heat on already wired deer and bust them out of there. It's better to back off 200 yards or so and set up on a ridge or point where you can cover several entry and exit routes into and out of a cover. Hunt the spot early and late, and again stick it out at midday if you have the time and the patience. You might score yet.

Funnels and Fringes

One year David Hale, the game-call maker from western Kentucky, leased 1000 acres that bordered a huge tract of timber-company land. He let two people bowhunt the woods in October, but they saw neither big bucks nor big sign. They didn't go back.

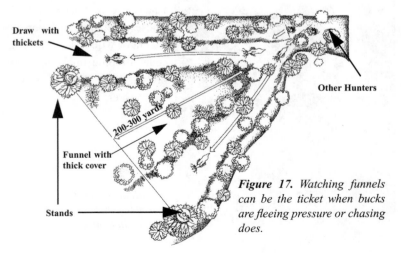

Draw with thickets

Other Hunters

200-300 yards

Funnel with thick cover

Stands

Figure 17. Watching funnels can be the ticket when bucks are fleeing pressure or chasing does.

"It was the first spot I hit when gun season opened," Hale told me.

It was the second Saturday in November and deer were chasing like mad. "We're lucky to be able to hunt the rut with a rifle," notes Hale. "Our gun season is short, 10 days, and we've got some good bucks running around this part of the country. Some other states are like that. It's a perfect time to be selective and hunt for a trophy."

Hale sneaked onto the 1000 acres and hung a tree stand at the top of a hollow, where he could watch three draws and finger ridges below. The draws were laced with strips and pockets of cedars, pines and honeysuckle, what Hale calls "fringe cover."

The sun rose and rifles cracked on the timber ground, where public hunting was permitted and heavy. Over the next couple of hours Hale spotted five wild-eyed bucks. Three of them chased does down the draws and over the ridges. The other two fled the nearby shooting and ran the funnels into the fringe thickets. At nine o'clock Hale shot a deer with a swollen neck and a rack that scored 157 inches.

His plan was a no-brainer.

"That timber land near my lease was full of old clear-cuts and planted pines," Hale says. "When all those hunters converged on the area, something had to give. I figured bucks would run out of there and down the draws and into the covers on my side of the fence. And by watching those funnels I was in good position for any rutting deer that came by."

To get lucky like that, try to set up on a private tract 200 yards to half a mile off a public border. Position a stand or blind on a ridge, at the head of a hollow, anywhere you might spot bucks crossing or re-crossing an area as they chase does or flee pressure. "Watch those fringe covers because that's where the big bucks will almost always go," adds Hale.

Public-Land Tactics

Suppose you don't have access to a small, private tract that teems with whitetails. Along with hundreds or even thousands of other people, you're forced to hunt deer on a national forest or state wildlife-management area near home. Well, when you set out to find a needle in a haystack—in this case a trophy buck on public ground—scouting is vitally important.

If you're a turkey hunter, start poking around a public area in the spring. As you look and listen for gobblers, cover lots of ground and keep an eye out for last fall's rubs, trails and scrapes. There are lots of clear-cuts and thinned-woods in a national forest; check for deer sign in and around the prime bedding areas. Come fall, some habitual does and bucks will use the same spots where you find old sign and cover.

Scour topo maps and aerial photographs for secluded ridges, flats or creek bottoms that the crowds might miss. Monitor access roads that have been gated and locked for years. If a public-land manager opens up a road this fall, few people might know about it. You can find some awesome hunting back in the newly accessible area.

The opening-week heat on any national forest or state area is intense. Your plan is simple. Hang a tree stand or set a ground blind in a good spot where you can see well, and sit in it most of the day, or all day. The plan has merit for two reasons.

Even though the rut is winding down when many gun seasons open, you never know when a buck will herd a last hot doe past your post. Secondly and more to the point here, think about what might happen when other guys climb out of their stands and hike back to their trucks around 10:00 each morning or stomp back to their blinds later that afternoon. That's right, one of the hunters might chase you a good buck.

On public land, sit in a stand all day long. Another hunter might drive you a buck anytime.

A hillside, ridge, knoll or bluff is a good vantage for an all-day post. Mast, green browse and especially thick cover nearby add to the allure of a setup. Try to watch a couple of funnels or edges below. That's where bucks will most likely travel, whether on natural movement or pushed by people.

Here are a few more tips to keep in mind:

- Drive the perimeters of a public area and look for trucks. Keep an eye out for tree stands and blinds in the woods. On a topo or aerial map, mark ridges and hollows where you heard the most shots on opening weekend. After patterning other hunters, slip into a secluded, thick spot and go for your buck.
- Take off work and hunt from Tuesday to Thursday, especially early in the season. Deer will use Monday to settle down a little bit from the carnival atmosphere of opening weekend, and most hunters won't be back until the following Friday or Saturday.
- Mature deer sneak around and hole up in multiple covers to elude hunters. A thicket might be empty for a while, but a big buck might show up there 4 or 5 days later. Keep watching.

Sanctuaries and Soft Pushes

Terry Drury is a deer-hunting machine. Each fall he hits Illinois, Iowa and Kansas, gunning for big bucks and footage for his Drury Outdoors video series. Like many folks these days, Drury hunts small to medium-size farms and woodlands. But instead of stomping over every inch of turf like most guys do during gun season, he sets aside 15- to 20-acre sanctuaries on each of his lands.

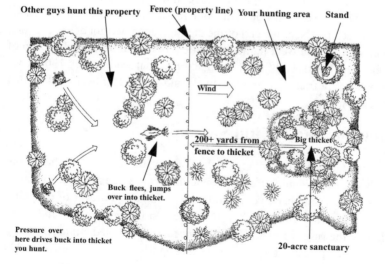

Figure 18. Designating part of your hunting land a "sanctuary" can draw bucks to you when hunting pressure heats up.

> **Quick tip:** Rifle or shotgun season on a public area is certainly not the best time to rattle or call, since whitetails are wired and off their normal movement patterns. Still, keep your horns, grunter and bleat call handy. If you spot a buck flashing over a ridge or through a thicket, crack the horns or make a call. He might pause briefly, so shoot fast if you can.

"What happens when gun season opens and people hike into stands, and start making drives on properties all around, and start shooting all over the place?" Drury asks. "Well, deer don't run out of the country, but they do head for non-pressured spots. If you designate a patch of timber or a thicket a sanctuary and stay out of it—no scouting, no stands, no nothing in there— deer will pile into it. It becomes sort of a holding area for bucks that seek cover from hunters not only on your land, but also from people swarming the adjacent grounds. Sometimes you can score big by hunting from stands overlooking food sources or doe trails on the fringes of a sanctuary."

Only as a last resort does Drury step foot into one of his sanctuaries. If he does go in, he makes only a soft push. He walks alone, and slowly and quietly through a cover. He sure doesn't want deer to bust out of there and jump a fence onto the next property where a line of hunters awaits. He just hopes a good buck will get up and sneak past a shooter and cameraman posted on the far edge of the sanctuary.

"We once stayed out of a 20-acre patch of timber for 7 years," Drury recalls. "Near the end of the eighth season, we got desperate for a buck on film. We went in, made a little push and moved 30 deer. Ten of them were bucks, and five of 'em had racks that would score 130 inches or better. My friend shot a good buck, and we haven't been back in that sanctuary since."

Bowhunting in Gun Season

It's a red-hot trend. Across the country, more and more hard-core archers are bowhunting during general firearms seasons. (It's legal in most states, but check your regulations.) To have a prayer of dropping the string on a good buck with hunters stomping around and rifles ringing the ridges and hollows, you need a well-honed strategy.

For starters, don't think about setting up where you can see 100 to 200 yards through the woods. Sure, a gun hunter might kick up a buck, but what are you going to do, sit there and watch him flag by well out of bow range?

Pack a tree stand on your back and sneak into a secluded thicket on a ridge or in a draw. Or hunt the edge of a dense swamp or clear-cut. Set up in a cover where your early-season scouting turned up doe trails, big rubs, tracks and scrapes. If acorns fall nearby, that's better yet.

Hang your stand high in a tree in the middle of cover. You might be able to see only 30 yards or so through the brush, but so what? That's as far as you can shoot. Climb up and hunt all day if you can hack it.

Sometime during the morning or afternoon, hunters on your land or on an adjoining property are apt to spook some does and drive them into your thicket. The gals might flash through, or they might stop to bed down or browse. Hopefully a good buck will follow them in there and step into an open shooting lane.

If you bow hunt during gun season, hang your stand in a thicket laced with deer trails. You might stick a buck fleeing pressure.

Big Bucks – Homeboys

Biologists in Illinois radio-collared and monitored 100 whitetails, including 38 bucks, on a large study area of cornfields, thickets and timber strips. When gun season opened, the deer stayed put and hopped around from standing corn to thickets to strips to elude hunters. Another

Blow grunts from the beginning of archery season through the end of gun season. You might pull in a buck anytime.

research project on a Missouri public area found that hunters often walked within 25 yards of pressured bucks, which flattened out and hid in thick cover.

The point: Reams of modern research confirm that whitetails don't hightail it for the next county when the guns start booming. Mature bucks hang in their core areas, stick to cover and move mostly at night. Hang tough, hunt hard and you can get one.

Chapter 11

Last-Chance Bucks

Come December you're dog-tired. For the better part of 3 months, you've gotten up early, real early, on weekends and off days. You've trucked hundreds or thousands of miles to hunting spots, scouted for every conceivable scrap of sign, wrestled with tree stands, sweated in the heat, shivered in a cold rain or snow, spooked some does and bucks, and maybe missed a huge deer. All of that is tough on both the body and the brain and enough to make you want to lock away your bow or gun and bark, "That's it. I'll get 'em next year."

You started scouting back in September. Well, keep it up. You've got to stay hot on the trail of fresh buck sign if you expect to fill your last tag.

Man, that's the wrong attitude. Whitetail season is still going strong in December and January in many regions. Suck it up and keep hunting because there's still plenty of time to punch your tag.

The Late Rut

At first I figured a hunter on the next ridge had spooked the jittery, wide-eyed doe that dashed past my stand. But then I had this strange premonition. Was something more poignant happening here? I readied my rifle, just as a buck prowled through the thicket, grunting softly, his black-tipped nose scouring the ground. I calmed my nerves and pressed the trigger.

That would have been your classic rut hunt, except for one thing: I killed that gnarly 9-pointer on a cold day in the middle of December, nearly a month after the breeding season had peaked in Virginia.

Try as they might, mature bucks cannot impregnate all of a herd's does during the primary breeding phase in early to mid-November in most regions, or in December or mid-January in a few southern states. This is especially true today in the many places where the sex ratio of whitetails is way out of whack—say one mature buck for every five or more does. There simply aren't enough studs to service all those females the first time around.

© Charles J. Alsheimer

Hunters and biologists across the country report spotting more monsters than ever before seeking the last estrous does in late November and early December. Stay out there!

In central, eastern and southern states with adequate habitats and temperate climates, does missed by the bucks, as well as those that were bred but failed to conceive, enter second and sometimes even third and fourth estrous cycles in the winter. Of interest to most hunters is the doe-in-heat stage that occurs 24 to 28 days after the peak of the rut.

Contributing to what is commonly called the "late" or "second" rut is the puberty of female fawns. In regions where food is abundant and nutritious, biologists say that some 6- and 7-month-old does may be ready to breed by December or January.

When all those recycling does and precocious fawns begin swirling a second wave of estrous scent, the woods should once again erupt with wild-eyed, tongue-lolling bucks, right? Wrong. As compared to the frat-party atmosphere of the main rut, the late show is like a black-tie affair. Males and females commingle, but in a much more subdued manner. Heck, many years you'll see nary a hint of late-rutting activity.

Still, if bow or gun season is still open in your area, you need to be in the woods. Relatively few people are. Many hunters have already filled

their tags, while others have simply packed it in until next season. As the woods settle down, deer feel increasingly secure reverting to their bed-to-food patterns. After hol-

The latest research shows that some mature bucks go back and check old scrapes from November 19 to December 10. Hunt near reactivated scrapes.

ing up for a couple of weeks, some of the more aggressive bucks get cocky and begin skulking around in search of the last estrous does.

To spot one, go back and hunt the most active scrapes you found back in the pre-rut. Late in the season, some bucks reactivate some scrapes in areas where they hooked up with the first estrous does. Work a key ingredient—cover—into your strategy. Any big deer that survived a hail of arrows and bullets earlier in the season will reactivate scrapes in or around the gnarliest, most secluded thickets he can find. Don't go back and hunt the scrapes per se, but definitely hunt thick cover where a few scrapes have been reactivated.

Back to the Feed

During what we hunters call the post-rut, and what some biologists call the "recuperation period," does and bucks seek out the last best food sources, limited as they may be, to refuel their rut-thin bodies. If you hunt farm country, focus your efforts, especially in the evenings, around an old field of corn, soybeans or the like. Obviously the more feed left standing or scattered on the ground, the better.

A good strategy is to sacrifice a couple of your last hunting days of the year to scout. Mentally, that is a tough thing to do because you feel you ought to be out there going like hell and trying to fill your last tag. However, 2 or 3 days of low-impact glassing can pay off big-time.

Drive to a crop field around 3:00 one afternoon. Hide your truck behind a hill or in a bottom, out of sight and mind of deer. Hike to a vantage 400 yards or so off the field, bundle up in plenty of warm clothes,

In December your best chance for a giant is to hunt the edge of soybeans, corn or the like.

settle in and glass for deer coming to the feed. A procession of does will show first, followed, hopefully, by a buck or two at dusk.

The second you spot a good buck you'll want to glass his rack and gawk, glass and gawk some more … but why? You already know he's a shooter, so get down to business before all the light is gone.

Where exactly did the buck pop out of the brush or timber? You need to know, for that will help you draw a line to his bedding area. Where might that be? I find that late in the season, many bucks seek shelter on the first east- or south-facing slope off a field, where they curl up close to the feed and out of the bitter west or northwest wind. Check for that ridge or grassy hillside on a topo map or aerial photo.

An old buck might vary his approach from a ridge to a field every afternoon, but if he pops out of the same corner or edge 2 or 3 days running, perfect! You've patterned the deer as best you can. Now you're ready to head over to the field the next day and hang a tree stand or set up a ground blind.

When you go for one last crack at a buck, you'd better get the wind right. The breeze obviously can't blow back toward a trail or bedding cover in the timber, and it can't swirl out into a field where the does will

pop out first. Strive to set up on a field edge where your scent will blow across and back into a dead zone in the timber where no deer will come out. If just one doe winds

Whitetails are super-wired late in the season. Play the wind and hide behind terrain and trees as you still-hunt or sneak to a stand.

you and starts stamping and blowing, you probably won't see your buck that night. Heck, you might never see him again.

Since whitetails are stressed and wired late in the season, access to your stand or blind is critical. You've got to slip into and out of a field-side post without deer seeing you. If you can't use a ditch, deep creek bank or thick brush to cover your moves, don't risk it. If you bump one doe back in the barren timber, you'll spook a bunch of deer. They'll blow out of the area, and they'll probably change their bed-to-feed pattern. Switch to Plan B and try to figure out a better way to access the field and get close to your target buck.

OK, you finally get the wind and access right. You stand on the edge of a field, scratch your head and try to decide where to set up. Keep in mind that a buck will often step out into a field upwind of where most does spill out of the timber. That way the buck can see and smell what's in front of him while the does cover his backside. So outfox Mr. Big by hanging your stand or setting your blind close to where he'll step out into the feed and above the does.

Many of you hunt private or public woodlands, where the nearest corn or bean field is miles away. Still, you ought to go back and hunt the feed—the "secondary feed." Every woodlot has some.

Scout an area where you found big rubs and scrapes early in the season. If you find huge tracks in mud or snow, a "hawg" like this is still working the area. Keep hunting him!

Begin by scouting a ridge, draw or creek bottom where you found big rubs and scrapes earlier in the season. If you find a single set of huge tracks in the mud or snow, or big prints mixed in with a bunch of doe tracks, you can figure a good buck is still working the area.

Now scour the nearby woods for the last scraps of food. Deer paw through piles of leaves or snow to get at wild apples, cherries, acorns, beechnuts or any other old mast they can find.

Also, check your maps for a 2- to 4-year-old cutover, burn or pine plantation in the area. A regenerating thicket provides great cover for skittish bucks. Also, enough sunlight filters through in spring and summer to grow honeysuckle, greenbrier and all sorts of other browse for deer to nibble on.

The edges of power lines, beaver swamps and the like are also good places to hunt. The fringes hold honeysuckle and other browse, and they also provide good cover for bucks ghosting around at dusk and dawn.

When you go about hanging a tree stand or setting a ground blind, be sure to get the wind right, just as you would when hunting a field. Again, access your post smartly. Skirt bedding areas and try not to spook a single deer on your way in or out.

During the post-rut, a super-hungry buck feeds heavily at dusk and during the night. But since a big deer feels somewhat safe and hidden back in the timber or in a thicket, he might well get up and browse buds and stems or nose for old acorns at 10 A.M., noon or 2 P.M. You never know. Hang tough and hunt with confidence all day. Since you've gone back to the feed, you've got a good chance to fill your last tag.

I favor a cedar or brush blind in December. It offers great cover, and you'll be warmer on the ground than in a tree stand.

One Last Still-Hunt

Over the course of a season, you might spend 20 or 30 days in a tree stand. To break the monotony and possibly the ice, why not try a little still-hunting late in the year?

Pick a rainy day when the woods are quiet. The morning after a light snow is best. You can pad along like a ghost and maybe cut a fresh track. An old, gray buck up ahead will pop out like a neon sign against the white backdrop.

Stay high on a ridge or hillside, but don't skyline. Creep slowly and pause every few steps behind trees. Glass down into draws and bottoms. Only the hardiest brush and vegetation are standing now. Dissect every inch of it with your binocular. Look for a piece of a deer—a flickering ear or tail or, best of all, a tine shining in the soft winter sunshine.

A few years ago some guys in my hunt club put on a last-ditch drive. Hearing them coming a mile away, I formulated a quick plan, which is easy to do when you hunt on foot.

The drivers moved east through a beaver swamp. I stayed high and still-hunted in the same direction. Soon I heard deer running in the leaves. Five does and an 8-pointer churned up a draw a half-mile from the drivers and 80 yards from me. My 30-06 roared. I walked to the buck and checked my watch—two o'clock on the last Saturday of the season. Now that's what I call taking it down to the wire.

Nudge A Buck

Eliot Strommen stuck his thick hand into the darkness and pointed down toward the river. "Your stand is 100 yards right through there." Strommen, a big man who glides through the timber like a deer, turned to leave, then jogged back and whispered, "Oh yeah, I almost forgot. Get ready about ten o'clock. Watch west."

I found the stand in the cottonwood tree without too much trouble. Some whitetails moved early, then nada. I was in the midst of one of those mind-wandering lulls when things heated up.

From out of the west, a dozen does slipped toward my stand ... a 6-pointer ... a thin-antlered 8-point ... and finally a 150-inch bruiser! As the big 10-point quartered past, I pulled my bow and grunted. He stopped, 18 steps away, his lungs smack behind a thick limb! The buck eased off into the brush and broke my heart. I checked my watch—10:05 A.M.

Though I had caught a bad break, Strommen's plan had worked to perfection. He had moved that buck into cake-shooting range from nearly a mile away. Was I impressed? You bet. Surprised? Nah. Nudging big deer to his buddies and clients along the Milk River in Montana is the big man's specialty.

Outfitter Strommen's approach to driving deer is unconventional— and perfect for these modern times. "We never walk from one end of a cover to the next like most guys do, spooking deer and watching them run all over the place," he told me. "We just nudge a buck from one small cover to the next cover or the next. It's a great way to move deer anytime, and especially late in the season."

Start out by putting a buddy in a block or strip of timber a half-mile or farther from where you'll start a push. Make sure the shooter watches a trail or funnel in the cover. Your goal is to move a buck a long way to a secondary cover where he feels safe. You want the deer to pick up a trail or funnel and trickle undisturbed by your buddy.

To make it happen, you need to know your country and your deer. Strommen has lived and hunted along the Milk River all his life. He's spent countless hours glassing whitetails in the wheat and alfalfa fields. He's watched deer weave into and out of the cottonwoods and brush, and cross the gray river a million times. "If I move a nice buck, I know where he'll go," Strommen says. "If he doesn't stop in the next cover, I know the third or fourth one he'll go to."

Plan a 2- or 3-man nudge for a buck. Any more hunters than that is often too many.

The point: Before you nudge, glass and pattern deer as best you can. Scout like a wild man, keying into food sources, bedding areas and the escape routes that link them.

You should always work a farm or woodland from the outside in. You sure don't want to drive a monster buck off your property at the end of the season. Walk outer thickets first, and move toward the center of your hunting area where your shooter is posted.

Don't worry too much about the wind. Just walk nonchalantly through a thicket or patch of brushy timber where deer typically bed. Walk out in the open and hope deer see you.

The minute you jump a good buck, slow down, way down. Once a big deer gets up, he'll move to a secondary cover, but if he's not too rattled, it might take him 20 minutes or longer to get there. Don't push him.

Here's another cool thing that Strommen taught me: Let whitetails do most of the work for you. Say you nudge 10 deer into a brushy strip where 10 other deer are bedded. Stop and wait for a while. Whitetails are like cattle. If one animal gets nervous and breaks for the next cover, the other 19 are likely to follow. If there's a nice buck in the bunch, your hunter might get a shot if he's set up in the right spot.

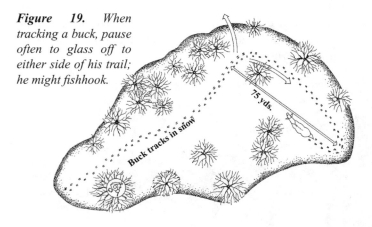

Figure 19. When tracking a buck, pause often to glass off to either side of his trail; he might fishhook.

75 yds.

Buck tracks in snow

Quick Tip: If you cut a big, smoking track in soft snow, follow it. When you see by the buck's stride that he is slowing down, stop and glass carefully. Check as far as you can out front, and 100 yards off to each side of the trail, since the old boy might have sensed you following and fish-hooked. Try to spot him before he sees you and spooks.

Last Shots

- Hang a bow stand as high as you feel safe and comfortable, and set it against cover—limbs with the last brown leaves, vines or the like. When a buck cruises below, draw, glue a sight pin low on his heart/lung vitals and release. Even the quietest bow will twang a bit, and the wired deer will likely duck right into the arrow's plane, which should make for a nice middle-of-the-lungs shot.
- Hunting with a rifle, slug gun or muzzleloader, take the first good poke you get at a buck. If you tarry, waiting for a big deer to come 10 yards closer or turn this way or that, he'll get away. You probably won't see him again until next fall—if you ever see him again.

Post-Season Scouting

Most of the best big-buck hunters I know scout a lot in January, February or March. You ought to also, and here's how to go about it.

On a day when there is no snow on the ground, drive to your best hunting area, park your truck and start walking. Cover every inch of turf and look for big rubs, rub lines, scrapes and trails that you might have missed last season. The sign is easy to spot in the barren winter woods. Mark it all on a map. If the terrain and food sources remain the same, habitual does and bucks will travel and rut in the same general areas next fall.

As you poke around the woods, look for the coolest relic of all. Your best shot at finding a shed antler is around a winter food source where many deer congregate, but you might also stumble across one in a nearby bedding thicket. In reality, an antler is liable to fall off a buck's head anywhere, so sheds are where you find 'em.

Modern Gear Tip: Wear a sweater or fleece pullover or vest lined with Gore's WindStopper fabric. The high-tech stuff works wonders for blocking a bone-chilling wind, allowing you to put in extra time on stand late in the season. Cabela's sells a good selection of Mossy Oak camouflage lined with WindStopper.

Say you get lucky and pick up one side of a massive 8-point rack one day. Or you hit the jackpot and find the matching sheds of a 150-inch buck. You now know that deer survived the previous hunting season. As you stand there and gawk at the piece of bone, you know you're

My buddy found this antler one February day in the 60-acre woods behind his house. He shot the buck 100 yards from this spot one afternoon the next November.

somewhere in the buck's home range, and quite possibly smack in the middle of his core area. The big deer will be back next fall. So should you.

Chapter 12

Backyard Bucks

My friend Rick has a den full of mounts that will make your jaw drop. When guys come over to play poker or shoot a little pool, they ogle the 130- to 160-inch racks and ask, "Man, where'd you shoot that one? And that one? What about that 10-pointer, he's a hawg!"

They seem stunned when my friend smiles, points out back and says, "Right there."

Rick is not only a good hunter, but also a smart hunter. He has figured out that to kill a good buck these days, you don't have to blow the kids' college funds or your 401K on a road trip to Alberta or Texas. Rick shells out $50 a year for a resident hunting license, and a couple hundred bucks for arrows, broadheads, Pyrodex, 270 shells and other basic gear. In September he hangs a couple of tree stands on his 60-acre property, a patchwork of fields, thickets and oak woodlots. He hunts like a wild man with bow and gun in October and November when he can get off work. And he shoots some eye-popping bucks. You ought to see his latest wall-hanger—a 10-pointer with 6-inch bases and an 18-inch inside spread.

You might not have the luxury of walking out your back door and hunting mature bucks like Rick, but for many hunters who live east of the Mississippi River, the crack at a trophy is just a short drive away. These days a bunch of Pope and Young whitetails, and even some Booners, live like kings under our noses. Here's how to find them and hunt them in three typical modern habitats.

The Woodlot

Ten to 50-acre home or building lots in towns, suburbs and fast-developing rural areas hold lots of whitetails—45 or more per square

© Charles J. Alsheimer

These days, think small for big deer. Some awesome bucks inhabit 20-acre lots and 50-acre timber blocks.

mile in many areas. Biologists say you'll find the healthiest bucks with the biggest racks in habitats with fewer than 30 deer per square mile. The best lots are diverse, mostly hardwoods interspersed with thickets, a few stands of pines or cedars and maybe a creek or two.

Figure 20. "Lot" Bucks — know where deer bed in lots and feed. Access stand accordingly so as not to chase deer out of the lots.

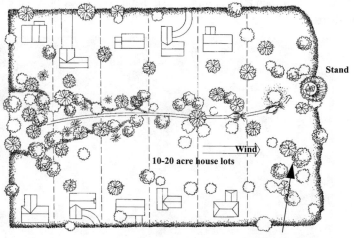

Dogs bark, kids yell, commuters fire up their SUVS, and whitetails could care less as they walk across driveways and browse fruit trees and shrubs. But the animals are still wild and unpredictable. If you spot a good buck and drive or walk away from him, he might just stand there; but make a sudden move toward the deer and he'll probably flag and run, just like a whitetail in a deep-woods environment.

Also, "lot" bucks smell all sorts of stuff—car exhaust, burgers on the grill, trendy suburban guys puffing on cigars—on the developed fringes of their habitats, but you'd better wear a scent-blocker suit and play the wind when scouting, hanging tree stands and hunting inside a woodlot or big thicket behind your house. Too much human stink inside a mature buck's core area can and will drive him to a secondary hiding place.

In this type of habitat, a buck's home range may encompass 25 to 50 or more lots that sprawl across one segment of a county. That is something many hunters fail to take into account, but you need to. Job one is to pin down when and where a good buck feeds, beds or simply passes through the lot you're hunting.

In September or October, check for a couple of white or red oaks dropping acorns in your lot. Look around for strips and pockets of green browse, like honeysuckle. Since lots are small, forget about trying to find and decipher rub lines into the mast or browse. Just look for clusters of rubbed trees—the bigger the better—on an oak ridge or flat. Deep, splayed, 3- to 4-inch tracks seal the deal that a good buck or two are feeding there.

To whack a "lot buck" in October, scout for a cluster of rubs and fresh tracks near a hot oak tree, then sneak in and set up downwind.

Look inside a lot for a half-acre swamp, a ridge thicket, a weedy ditch because it doesn't take much cover to hide a big buck. Check a bedding site for large tracks and droppings, and jump for joy if you find one or two rubs as thick as your leg. That's the best sign yet that a big-racked deer is hanging in a lot.

Scout for deer trails that link acorns and thickets. Note "freeway trails" that simply cut through a lot and run onto and off adjacent properties. You'll find many deer runs on the tops and sides of ridges, and in hollows and creek bottoms.

The big challenge is to slip into a lot without chasing deer out and blowing your hunt each day. Be smart and devise an entry/exit plan. Suppose there's a huge thicket three quarters of a mile to the west of a stand you hung near a highly productive oak tree. On afternoons after work, play the wind and sneak into the spot from the east or south. You won't bump deer coming to the acorns from their bedding area. Same thing on morning hunts. Predict where deer feed and mingle at night—maybe in a corn or alfalfa field three properties over—and take an off-side route into a bedding-area stand the next morning.

In November, or December or January down South, watch those freeway trails that cut through lots. Rank bucks run them to scent check and pick up does, often cutting through and across 10 lots or more. When archery hunting in a town or suburb, play the wind and hang a stand 25 yards off a run. If it's legal and safe to hunt with a muzzle-loader, shotgun or even a 270, back 70 yards or so off a trail, and try to set up where you can cover two or more runs. You're apt to nail that big 8–pointer that you spotted back in October, or a strange bruiser cruising your lot for girls.

The Timber Block

In suburbs and rural areas 40 miles or so outside cities, 50- to 200-acre blocks of woods can be awesome places to hunt whitetails. They are small enough to concentrate and funnel lots of deer, yet large enough for multiple stand sites that you can hunt on different winds. Many linear strips of timber are dotted with thickets and connect crop fields, pastures or larger woodlands, and that just makes things better.

Timber blocks are larger than the woodlots we just talked about, so some deer spend a lot of time in them, munching acorns, browsing or loafing in thickets. Other nonresident does and bucks cruise through the woods en route to feeding and bedding areas. Whatever the case, a block may be only an eighth or a quarter of a buck's home range, so you need to find out when he's in the woods you're hunting, or at least when he'll amble through.

To do it, speed scout your block one day in September or early October, checking for falling acorns, green browse and the like. Look around for loafing and bedding thickets, the edges of which may be blazed with rubs. You might find a rub line wending from a thicket to an oak tree or a crop field that borders the timber. Or you might not find one. It really doesn't matter because you can surmise that a lot of deer will move between the thickets and the food sources.

Set a few tree stands to overlook edges, hollows, ridge points and creek bends and crossings where the animals ought to travel. Inside any block of timber anywhere in America, mature bucks walk along edges, down funnels and around points, especially those rimmed with cover. As you sneak into your spots each day, be on the lookout for any fresh rubs, tracks and scrapes that may pop up. You often need to tweak your stand placement a bit to set up a shot at a buck.

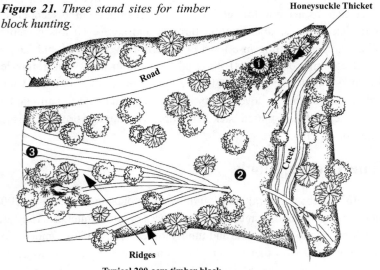

Figure 21. *Three stand sites for timber block hunting.*

Honeysuckle Thicket

Road

Creek

Ridges

Typical 200-acre timber block.

Since deer move into and out of timber blocks all the time, coming and going and cutting across, your funnel stands are apt to produce either in the morning or afternoon. Carefully access your stands and play the wind so you'll spook as few deer as possible on the hike in or out. Hunt the perches on a rotational pattern every few days to minimize your scent and presence in an area.

When the rut erupts, a buck will probably leave your block. Heck, you might spot a big deer you've been hunting all bow season chasing a doe across a road or pasture 2 miles away. But hang tight, especially if you're seeing does every day. While he's gone another 8- or 10-pointer might cruise past one of your stands, hot after those untended ladies. There's a great chance the big boy you really want will circle back into his home core area. You might get him yet.

Play the wind and hide behind terrain and cover on the way to and from a stand. Try not to push a single deer out of your lot or timber block.

The Small Farm

Crops, pastures, thickets, woodlots, creeks … These days, hunters are shooting many Pope & Young whitetails on farms with, say, 200 to 600 acres of prime mixed habitat. Some Boone & Crockett bucks prowl these modern haunts.

Once a symbol of rural America, many farms are dwindling in size as suburbs continue to sprawl into the country. You might drive past one of the big-buck hotspots every day on your way to work. If you think that may be the case, try to get permission. Round up a few friends, pay a lease fee and implement a simple but effective deer-management plan if you can. You'll have awesome deer hunting for years to come.

These days, some of the best deer hunting is on 200- to 500-acre farms. Try to lease and manage one.

What more could a buck want? On a small to mid-size farm, he has food, cover and does at his beck and call. Why would he go anywhere else? If you keep the hunting pressure relatively light, a big deer will live there year-round.

In this type of habitat, deer are accustomed to seeing and hearing cars and farm trucks. They're used to people feeding cows, mowing hay, cutting wood, etc. inside their covers. Like they do in all checkerboard habitats, old bucks become masters of deception by hiding in thickets and moving a lot at night. There are plenty of good bucks here, but they are no pushovers to hunt.

On September evenings, a few days before archery season, glass the edges of a corn or soybean field for a trophy coming to feed and show-boat for does. Study where the big guy comes out of the surrounding woods. Then one day at lunchtime, hustle over to the edge and hang a tree stand for an ambush.

Try to stick a buck from a field-side perch in early fall, when he's still on a predictable bed-to-feed pattern. If you don't get him by the time blackpowder or modern gun season rolls around, you'll probably have to head back into the bordering woods.

Sneak in there, without spending too much time and laying down too much scent, randomly looking for big rubs and tracks. You know the buck is close by, but where? A perimeter thicket on a ridge a half-mile or so from a crop field is a good place to start looking. The buck may bed there, or he might stage in the cover before hitting the field after dark.

Now sneak in on a pointed mission and check the edges of a thicket for big rubs, scrapes and tracks. Check for freshly falling acorns, which help to hold does and bucks in a small area. Look for a nearby hollow, saddle or similar funnel pocked with sign. Play the wind and set a stand, like I did a couple of years ago.

One November morning I spotted a deer, fat as a steer, tipping up out of a beaver swamp, pushing through honeysuckle toward my ridge stand. I'd know those antlers anywhere! I'd seen the 9-pointer three times from my field sets back in archery season. I didn't want him to get away this time. BOOM! I fired my muzzleloader and dropped him with a 250-grain bullet. I couldn't claim his 140-inch rack for the record book, but who cared? He was a cool trophy, a homeboy I tagged less than 20 miles from my house.

Hunt Early

I live an hour outside the concrete jungle of northern Virginia, one of the fastest-growing regions in the United States. Suburbia is sprawling into the once-rural counties I roamed as a boy. New roads, houses and office buildings are going up everywhere—and so is the deer kill. Hunters tag a whopping 5000 to 6500 whitetails in the developing counties each season.

A good portion of the harvest occurs from early October through early November, during our archery and muzzleloader seasons. I think these are the best weeks to hunt small lands, especially lots and

Try to get your buck during an early archery or muzzleloader season, before the gun hunters swarm the woods.

timber blocks in moderately populated areas. Deer cling to late-summer patterns, and they're still fairly predictable in their travels between feeding and bedding sites. Even when bucks start scraping around Halloween, they stay home. They don't roam off a property like they often do during the peak of the rut.

Also, while mature bucks are used to seeing, hearing and smelling people on the fringes of their chopped-up habitats, they haven't been spooked badly by rifle or shotgun hunters inside their living quarters. In short, they haven't turned completely nocturnal yet. The takeaway lesson: Hunt a small property early and hard, and try to score before the hoards of rifle or slug gun hunters swarm the woods.

Last-Minute Bucks

As Cat D-9s rip roads and home sites in old farms and once-rural woodlands, a ton of edge cover and thickets are created. That is a big reason why whitetail populations are busting at the seams in many developing areas. Deer love to walk and browse in these strips, especially late in the season once acorns and other food sources have dried up.

If you don't score early, move one of your stands to the thickest, greenest edge you can find, and then watch for a buck skulking around at dawn or dusk on a December or January day. You might tag out yet in or near your backyard.

All Eyes and Ears

Each day as you drive to work or to a convenience store for a gallon of milk, look for whitetails milling in fields, crossing roads, etc. And keep your ears open. Mail carriers, meter readers, kids waiting for the bus … You just never know who'll brag about the big buck they just saw.

One day in November of 2002, your typical modern deer hunter Ben Brogle of Lancaster, Ky., was out hunting near home. Brogle's cousin told him about a "good buck" he had seen on a property just a couple of hours before. Brogle hustled over there, hunted the spot and shot the buck with his 243. The 36-pointer gross-scored 244 B&C points! When the final drying of the rack and the official scoring is done, the Brogle buck might be the new non-typical Kentucky record. See what you might get by keeping you ears open?

To gain access to spots where you saw a big deer or heard of one hanging out, put on civilian clothes and a smile and start knocking on doors. Face it, some people won't let you hunt, but many suburbanites and farmers will give you permission, especially if deer are eating up their azaleas, fruit trees or crops. If you're a bowhunter, say so. Some folks are leery of rifles cracking on their property, but they don't mind archery hunting.

Try to obtain permission to hunt several small tracts. If you can swing it, offer a lease fee and lock up the sole hunting rights. Then you can "cover hop" around and refrain from over-hunting your stands, thus minimizing the pressure you put on bucks. And you won't have to deal with other hunters.

Cover Pushes

Whitetails in small, broken habitats have small home ranges. Bucks seek shelter in many different woodlots or thickets within those 500 or 600 acres, and they know their bedding areas like the back of their hoof. You can take advantage of that.

One day, slip into one of your best tree stands. An hour later, have a buddy walk through two or three nearby lots or thickets where you have permission. It's not really a drive, just a good way to get bucks up and moving. A big deer might sneak out of a woodlot a half-mile away and sneak into a thicket where you're set up. When he gets there, he won't be spooked, since your buddy is not dogging him. Besides, the deer is used to cover-hopping to avoid people most every day. He might saunter under your stand and give you a shot. Moving deer in small covers is not just an end-of-the-season, last-ditch tactic. If you're smart about it, you and a buddy can nudge bucks to one another anytime during bow or gun season.

Quick Tip: It's more important than ever to take good shots and kill deer cleanly with one broadhead or bullet to the heart/lung vitals. A friend of mine recently tracked an 8-pointer for a mile. When he found the buck, some guy was gutting it! How anybody could claim another person's deer is beyond me, but strange things are happening as more and more people hunt small farms and woodlands. Put in extra time at the 3-D or rifle range, and strive to drop bucks within 100 yards or so of your stands. That way, you won't have to worry about a deer running off, crossing a fence and falling dead on a neighboring property where you might not have permission.

On a small property you're best off in a tree stand. You don't move around and spook bucks. You can monitor not only the deer, but also the movements of other hunters. Know the location of all roads, houses and barns, and never fire a gun in those directions.

Safe Shots

If you carry a centerfire rifle, or even a shotgun or a muzzleloader, on a small lot or farm, hunt from a tree stand, where you'll shoot down and toward the ground at bucks. Pay close attention to roads, houses, barns or livestock in the area. Never fire in those directions.

Chapter 13

Whitetail Myths & Misconceptions

How far does an old buck travel? Where does he bed? How does the moon's phase, pull or glow affect his rutting behavior? Ask 100 people and you'll likely get 100 different answers. And since many deer hunters are slow to change their ways, many of their responses will be rooted in the lore and half-truths of a bygone era. Well, it's time to bring your thinking—and hunting strategies—up to date. Let's do it by blowing holes in some popular whitetail myths and misconceptions.

The biggest myth of all is that a monster like this roams for miles and miles. The truth is, most big deer these days are homeboys.

> **MYTH:** Big bucks roam for miles and miles.
> **FACT:** Mature deer are homeboys.

For 4 years Jimmy Riley watched a buck grow from a "nice deer" to a shooter to a world-class animal.

"We always spotted that buck on the same 500-acre stretch of the island," says Riley, one of the head guides at Giles Island Hunting Lodge near Natchez, Miss. "Man, was he smart. He gave our guides and clients fits."

One December afternoon Riley climbed into a stand near a food plot, and waited. Just before dark he looked up and shivered. It was the big deer, coming straight in! Riley drew his bow and loosed an arrow. The 10-pointer with awesome mass and lots of kickers scored 173 $^6/_8$—the new No. 2 non-typical archery kill in Mississippi.

On Mississippi's Giles Island, many mature bucks live within 400 to 500 acres. It's like that across the country.

From the tale of Riley's giant buck, hone in on this quote: "We always spotted that buck on the same 500-acre stretch" of the 10,000-acre island. In areas with plenty of nutritious food sources and good numbers of does, the home ranges and core areas of mature bucks are smaller—much smaller—than most hunters think. That seems to be the case not only in the South and East, but also across the country.

"On my Iowa farm, a mature buck's home core area is usually only 200 to 300 acres," says my friend

Don Kisky, a whitetail fanatic with a wall of racks (including a couple of 200-inchers!) that will make your jaw drop. "And get this. I find that some old bucks spend most of their time in a few acres within their core areas."

For three decades Eliot Strommen has observed and studied whitetails on the ranches he owns and leases along the fertile Milk River in northeastern Montana. Out in Big Sky Country, you might think bucks roam far and wide. Well, think again.

"If they are not disturbed, most of our big deer—I'm talking about bucks that score 150 to 165 inches or more—live year-round within a range of a quarter to a half mile," says Strommen, who hunts and guides bowhunters most every day from September through November. "During the rut, which peaks around November 19 out here, a big deer that we haven't seen before might show up on one of our ranches, or a buck we're hunting might leave and go looking for does for a few days. But when all is said and done and the rut is over, the big bucks come back home."

The bottom line, and a recurring theme of this book: If you hunt a diverse habitat with lots of food, cover and water, does and mature bucks will live right there year-round. You won't have to go far to hunt a big rack.

MYTH: Bucks bed in the thickest cover available in an area.

FACT: Big deer sometimes bed out in the open where they can see a long ways.

Sometimes big deer bed out in the open, especially during the rut. Be careful and ready as you sneak toward a stand.

It's a no-brainer that mature bucks like the thick stuff, especially when the gun hunting heats up late in the season. But in early fall and during the rut, don't overlook bucks that bed in thin cover on ridges, bluffs, flats and points. The deer curl up, backs to the wind, and watch for does and other bucks (or predators) approaching from afar and below.

Ah, but you don't always have to look high. You might find a big deer holed up in a ditch, fallen treetop or tiny thicket out in the middle of a flat, open woodland.

You need to remember that as you still-hunt or sneak into a tree stand or blind each afternoon. Go slow into the wind, use your binocular and check out potential bedding sites up ahead and off to the sides. You might find Mr. Big where you least expect it.

MYTH: Fresh scrapes every 50 to 100 yards tell you a good buck is working a ridge or bottom.
FACT: That's likely the sign of a young buck feeling his oats.

"You'll think you've found the mother lode, but all those scrapes might be the work of an aggressive 1 ½- or 2 ½-year-old buck," says Terry Drury, who hunts and videos trophy whitetails across the Midwest. "We find that mature deer make big scrapes, sometimes half the size of a truck's hood, but they generally don't make as many scrapes as young bucks do."

If a ridge or funnel is hot during the rut, hang a stand and hunt it day after day. The day deer activity wanes, move to a fresh spot.

Check for a mangled licking branch above a scrape, as well as a "signature track" in the freshly pawed soil. "That print can tell you if the buck at work is mature or immature," notes Drury. "If you see a long, fat pad in a scrape, you're probably onto a good deer."

> **MYTH:** Don't overhunt a tree stand or blind.
> **FACT:** Often it pays to hunt the same spot several days in a row.

One October evening a buddy of mine dragged a 150-class buck into our Montana camp. "I was in that corner stand down by the alfalfa, and three other good bucks slipped by just out of bow range before I shot this one," he told me. "Man, that spot is hot. I bet you could go back there tomorrow and whack one, too."

The next day I climbed into the corner perch and drilled a 140-inch 9-pointer. How cool was that? Two Pope & Young bucks from the same stand in less than 24 hours.

When whitetails are locked into a bed-to-feed pattern early or late in the season, don't think twice about bowhunting a stand two or three days in a row if the wind stays right, and if you can slip into and out of the area without spooking too many deer. Conditions won't stay good forever, so strike while the iron is hot.

Also, don't worry too much about overhunting a spot during the rut, even if you're hunting with a gun. Deep in the Saskatchewan bush one November morning, Troy Ruiz, a producer for Mossy Oak's Hunting the Country TV show, and I climbed into a ground blind. The sun came up and we gazed out over our spot. Little poplar ridges and draws rolled away for 200 yards. Swamps and thick spruce bordered the thin timber all around. It was a perfect spot for a big deer to prowl out of the cover and go trolling for does.

> **Quick Tip:** An old-timer might have taught you to slit the throat and remove the hocks of the bucks you kill. Well, forget about it! That not only makes a big mess, it can also taint the venison. Simply field-dress a buck from stern to brisket. Hang a deer in the shade or a walk-in cooler, and skin it as quickly as possible. In these uncertain times of Chronic Wasting, Lyme and other diseases, always wear rubber gloves when whittling on a whitetail.

An hour into the sit, one did. A pig of a 9-pointer cruised up out of a draw and sniffed his way along a ridge. My 270 cracked and the buck went on a spectacular death run, crashing through the trees and snapping a couple of poplars in half before falling.

For a couple of hours, we admired the 150-inch buck and shot our closing segments. Then Mark, our guide, rumbled in with an ATV and loaded the buck for the trek out.

The next morning we were back in our blind at sunrise. Troy wanted to film more scenic shots of the spot, and we might even video a few more deer.

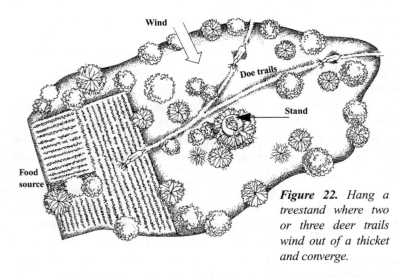

Figure 22. *Hang a treestand where two or three deer trails wind out of a thicket and converge.*

An hour into the sit, a doe popped over a ridge top, looking back and panting. Uh, oh. Here he came, head down and grunting like a market hog. The 14-pointer, which we figured would score in the 160s, nosed the doe round and round for 5 minutes. Troy's video of that buck is spectacular also.

To recap, the day before I had shot a buck with my 270. The 300-pound deer had crashed away for 75 yards, banging and cracking trees. We had spent 2 hours stomping around in the timber spot, laughing and talking and shooting video footage. An ATV had motored in and out of there. So what? The rutting 160-incher that showed up outside our blind the second day wasn't the least bit fazed.

When a ridge, funnel or flat is hot during the rut, go back to the well again and again and again. You and your buddies might shoot one, two or more good bucks chasing does in and around the same spot.

> **MYTH:** Dominant bucks don't walk doe trails.
> **FACT:** You might shoot a giant deer on a doe run.

A lot has been written recently about bucks circling downwind through cover to scent-check doe trails. True, they do that a lot during the scraping phase in late October and early November in most areas. But earlier in the season, bucks often stroll down doe trails into and away from food sources. You know those two Montana brutes I told you about in the previous section? My pal and I nailed those deer as they walked the same doe trail into a field of lush, green alfalfa.

Also, later on during the peak of the rut, crazed bucks cut and cruise main trails all the time, scent-checking and looking for hot gals. Watching runs in secluded, timbered draws is a great strategy then.

> **MYTH:** Bucks head for the hills when the guns start booming.
> **FACT:** Bucks lie low in their core areas.

Many research projects have debunked the old notion that hunting pressure drives bucks from their home ranges and into the next county. For example, Missouri biologists monitored radio-collared whitetails on a public area with an average of 43 gun hunters per square mile. Now

Harold Knight killed this beauty deep in rifle season on a small farm. Hang tough and score!

that's pressure! They found that range-wise, bucks didn't drastically alter their movements in response to the human intrusion. They simply holed up in cover during daylight hours. And get this: The study went on to find that hunters often walked within 10 yards of hiding deer, some of them mature bucks.

In northern and central states, I believe the rut is most intense when the moon is full between November 1 and 15. Hunt enough at midday and you'll see some awesome bucks on the prowl.

If a posted woods or farm lies inside a buck's normal home range of 500 to 600 acres, he might surely go there when the guns start booming. But if you hunt a larger private or public area with no refuge in sight, that same buck will cling to cover and move mostly at night. A bit of good news is that you might see a flurry of deer movement at midday when most other hunters leave the woods. Hang in there till you score.

> **MYTH:** A full moon makes for poor hunting.
> **FACT:** Bucks go bonkers during the "rutting moon."

Your granddaddy might have told you something like, "Boy, those bucks ain't gonna move in this full moon, so stay home." Well, I hate to argue with Pops, but new research suggests that the second full moon after

© Charles J. Alsheimer

That 20-acre thicket behind your house ... that block of timber just down the road ... a friend's 100-acre "farmette" ... all great spots to find lots of deer and some mighty fine bucks these days.

the autumnal equinox (in most years, it's the big moon in November) might trigger the whitetail rut in northern and central states. I can't verify that, but I will suggest getting out there during the "rutting moon" and hunting for a whopper buck seeking a doe.

Remember the 150-inch bruiser I shot in Saskatchewan? And the 160-incher that showed up outside our blind the next morning? Well, a full moon hung in the sky like a big pizza pie on that hunt. When mature bucks are trolling and chasing, the rut overrides the moon.

The old-timers were right about one thing, however. Deer do move and breed a lot at night beneath the creamy "rutting moon." But after bedding awhile at daybreak, many mature bucks get up and prowl for does again. Try to ambush one at midday in a funnel or on a ridge back in the timber. Patient hunters who hang tough in their stands whack a bunch of big deer between 9:00 A.M. and 2:30 P.M. each season.

> **MYTH:** You have to hunt a remote area to tag a big deer.
>
> **FACT:** Today, lots of gnarly-racked bucks live under our noses.

We discussed this at length in Chapter 12, but it bears repeating because many hunters still figure they have to drive for hours and hike for miles to hunt big deer in remote spots.

The whims of the stock market and the economy aside, new roads, subdivisions and industrial parks continue to sprout up across the East, South and Midwest. Progress has its downsides, but deer habitat is not one of them. Small, chopped-up covers in developing areas provide excellent food, edge and cover for whitetails. That 20-acre woodlot behind your house … that strip of timber just down the road … a friend's 200-acre

My choice for whitetails is the 270 or 30-06 with a Federal Premium 130- to 150-grain load. I top my rifles with a 2X-8X or 3X-9X scope.

Field-dress a buck as soon as possible. Cart the deer off and hang it in the cool shade, or in a walk-in cooler.

"farmette" 10 miles away … All these places should hold lots of whitetails and at least one good buck. Get permission, do a little scouting and set a few stands. Boom, just like that you might nail a P&Y or even a B&C buck, blowing a gaping hole in another whitetail myth.

More Fallacies & Facts

FALLACY: You can't tell whether a buck or a doe left a big track.

FACT: In many areas, a mature doe and a 2 ½-year-old buck might leave a nearly identical print. But anywhere in the country, a really old buck's track is distinctive. It will be 3 to 4 inches long and, more importantly, noticeably wide and deep in mud or snow. If a buck is 4 or 5 years of age or older, his hooves will probably be chipped, curved or split.

> **Modern Gear Tip:** Ten or 20 years ago, you might have needed to handload ammunition to get the most out of your deer rifle. It's now a myth that handloads are more accurate than factory rounds. Modern, high-velocity loads from Federal, Winchester and Remington are excellent and improving all the time. I hunt mostly with Federal Premium. Running 130- to 150-grain loads through my 270 and 30-06 rifles, I can shoot 1 ½-inch groups at 100 yards all day long from a bench. That's all the accuracy you need and then some for whitetails. Always hunt with a top-notch bullet. The Nosler Ballistic Tip, Nosler Partition and Trophy Bonded Bear Claw bullets are my favorites for bucks.

Look closely and you can often see such distinguishing characteristics in a print.

Anytime you find big tracks but aren't sure whether a buck or a mature doe left them, scout further. Big rubs and scrapes in the vicinity of large tracks seal the deal that you are onto a good buck.

> **FALLACY:** When you see the first deer chasing, the rut is on.

FACT: The rut is close when you see small and middling bucks going gaga. But the majority of does aren't breeding until you see bucks 3-½ years and older up and moving in daylight hours. Still, you ought to be on stand when the young bucks chase because you never know when the first big deer will get up and go looking for does.

> **FALLACY:** Bucks always travel into the wind.

FACT: I'd like to have a hundred dollars for every big buck I've seen walking with a tailwind over the past 20 years.

Sure, it makes sense that deer quarter into the breeze when they can, using their powerful noses to detect and sort out danger and the smell of other animals. But when a big buck needs to get from Point A (bed) to Point B (feed or especially a hot doe) in a hurry, he'll often cheat the wind and take the shortest route. Remember that when you set up. Hunt where the wind is in your favor, but watch for a buck coming from any direction, especially during the rut.

Chapter 14

Big-Buck Dilemmas

One afternoon a buck strolls by and busts you in a tree stand, seemingly for no good reason. Some guy on an ATV tools through your best spot one morning at sunup. A big deer lays down a maze of rubs and scrapes; you hunt the sign for 2 weeks, never seeing the ghost. Well, stuff like that is part of the game. When you hunt for heavy-racked whitetails these days, you need to be flexible and troubleshoot common dilemmas.

> **People talk about scouting for rub lines and hunting near them early in the season, but how do you find the sign?**

As mentioned in Chapter 8, rubbed trees that link a buck's bedding area and food sources can be tough, if not impossible, to find in September or October when the ground foliage is thick and the leaves are still on the trees. Scout for clus-

Other hunters and ATVs in the woods are a fact of life in most areas these days. Put up with a little pressure and learn to use it to your advantage.

ters of big rubs first because they're easiest to find. Then check out from those signposts for smaller rubs that reveal a buck's travel route.

A buck's rub line between bed and feed can be tough to find. Scout out from a huge "sign post" for smaller rubs that wend through the woods. Don't overlook rubbed vines!

That's still a chore. Just do the best you can during the early bow or muzzleloader season, and then, once your hunting is over in late fall or winter, go back and scout your hunt zone for rub lines that were made 2 or 3 months ago. At that time they're pretty easy to see in the barren, open woods. Go to a cluster of big rubs and kneel down to look out across the woods. Any rubbed saplings will still shine, and you can start piecing them together.

Don't stop there, though. Walk rub lines to see how far they go, and how and where they connect thickets and fields or mast flats. Look for spots where rub lines cut creeks and run along the edges of thickets, swamps or sloughs. There's a good chance the same buck, or another buck, will blaze rub lines in the same general places next fall. Go back then and you ought to find fresh sign. If so, play the wind, hang a tree stand and hunt a buck on his bed-to-feed route.

> **People talk about hunting a mature buck near his bedding area, or in transition zones leading to or from it. But how do you know exactly where a big deer beds?**

Early in the season it's not all that hard to predict where a buck lies up. Check thickets within 200 to 400 yards of a crop field or acorn flat. Be careful as you scout. Sometimes a buck will hole up in cover tighter to the feed, within 100 yards of it.

As the rut approaches and finally erupts, you never know where a buck will bed. He might come from the west one afternoon and from the east or south the next day. Some of the biggest deer killed every year take hunters by complete surprise. A guy might shoot a 170-inch buck and holler, "I thought he was bedding over there, but he chased a doe behind my stand, so I turned around and shot him!" You hear stories like that all the time.

The best you can do is hang a tree stand in a spot where you can see far and wide, and cover the entry and exit routes to several potential bedding thickets. Think of it as an observatory post, like we talked about in Chapter 7. Spend a lot of time in that stand, especially early and late in the day. If you spot a good buck a couple times and his bedding pattern begins to emerge, move your bow or gun stand tighter to a thicket you know he's using.

Keep one thing in mind. Anytime of year, a big deer likes to bed high, where he can scan the woods below for does and predators. The wind and thermals are generally steady up there, so the animal feels somewhat secure. Check for reliable sign—big tracks and rubs—in cover on ridges, points, hillsides and benches. Scout the low-impact way, which is always best around a bedding area, by sneaking along and glassing the fringes of thickets for shiny, telltale rubs.

> **A buck is leaving a mother lode of big tracks, rubs and scrapes in an area, but darned if you can see him. When and where is the best time to catch the ghost moving in shooting light?**

Bucks 3 ½-years of age and older are night owls. You probably already know they prefer to prowl around, feed and check does under a cloak of darkness. But did you also know that you have a short window of opportunity—a week or so—to catch him on his hooves at sunrise?

Even though you might never have seen the buck you're hunting, you should be able to guess where he's bedding (use the advice in the above section). Then, a week or so before the rut gets rolling, set a tree stand downwind of a likely bedding thicket. Set that perch as tight as you dare to the cover, and hunt it the next few mornings.

To spot a good buck in the morning, hunt tight to his bedding area, but don't go in there.

Late in the pre-rut, a buck makes nightly forays to sniff does in his core area. He plans on being curled back in bed before daybreak, but you know how that goes. During a long night of partying, it's easy to stay out too late. Sometimes a buck loses track of time as he runs from doe to doe. One morning in the wee hours, a big deer may find himself sneaking frantically back toward his bed as the sun glimmers in the east. From a stand hung at the end of a trail or funnel that leads to his bedding thicket you might see him and whack him. Of course once the rut explodes you might catch a big deer on his hooves later in the morning, so don't head back to your truck too early.

> **You find big rubs and smoking scrapes the size of dozer tires on a ridge. You get all fired up, rush in and set a tree stand near the sign. You hunt for a week and never see a buck.**

The closer you hunt to sign, the more likely deer will see you walking into the spot, hanging a stand, hiking out, or whatever. Worse, the buck running the area might wind you. Your stand might be 25 to 50 yards downwind of a scrape, but a rutting buck is notorious for circling 100 yards or so farther downwind and scent-checking an area before he comes in. If you're too tight to his scrapes he might smell you, melt away into the brush and change his pattern. While you sit hunting and watching his old sign, he has moved on.

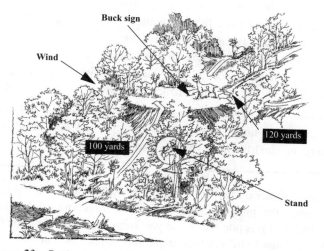

Figure 23. *Setting up too close to buck sign can cause a big deer to change his pattern. Back off!*

Look at it this way. If a stranger busted into your dining room or bedroom, you'd know it. Heck, you'd freak! On the other hand, if he hid out in a dark corner of a hallway you probably wouldn't see him, and you'd go about your routine. I believe you ought to hunt like that. Set up in cover 75 to 100 yards downwind of hot rubs, scrapes and trails on a ridge or in a bottom. The buck putting down the sign should not see or smell you sneaking in or hunting. He might stay on pattern so that you finally cross paths.

> **The sun is just beginning to glimmer in the east when some guy clumps by, or runs his ATV beneath your tree stand. You throw down your cap and cuss. Do you move or do you stay?**

On opening morning of muzzleloader season one fall, I was in my stand early and primed for action. I heard rumbling down through the woods. It was not an ATV, but a Ford F-150! The knucklehead drove down the power line I was hunting and parked 200 yards from my stand.

That morning I was so hot I climbed down and moved, but you don't always have to do that. Sure, a foot hunter or some guy on a quad might spook a buck that was mincing toward your post, but, then again, maybe not. A big deer might have been a mile away when the intruder came along.

As long as a hunter keeps walking or driving out of sight, calm down and sit tight. A buck might come along 30 minutes or an hour later.

Hunting pressure is a fact of life these days, so you need to learn to accept a certain level of it. If some guy hounds you two or three days in a row, however, pull your tree stand and get the heck out of the area. Go look for a quieter, more secluded place to hunt. You'll be safer, have more fun, and you probably stand a better chance of whacking an undisturbed buck.

You bump some deer, and possibly the old buck you've been hunting, on the hike in to your tree stand.

Busting deer on the walk into a morning stand is inevitable sometimes since the predawn is when both hunters and whitetails move around a lot. If it is pitch dark and you know the deer didn't wind you—maybe they just heard you walking in the leaves and scrambled away—continue on toward your stand. Hopefully it's close by and you won't walk through more deer. In the dark you won't know if a big buck was one of the deer that ran away, but it really doesn't matter. Climb quietly into your stand and wait for shooting light.

When you spook whitetails, they usually run off only a short ways. Does and maybe even a buck might mill around in the area all morning before they ease back over a ridge or through a funnel you're watching. And who knows, the big deer you're after might have been a mile away when you walked into the stand. He might stroll by an hour or two later, never realizing you're there.

Things are different when a buck sees you walking into a stand in the afternoon. He shouldn't smell you, since you should always approach a perch from a downwind angle. If you see a big-racked deer flag away, ease out the area and go hunt another spot that day. Come back in a couple of days and hunt the buck once he has settled down a bit.

Of course, it's best not to spook any deer at all. After setting any stand or blind, sit back and formulate an entry/exit plan. Evaluate trails, rub lines, scrapes and other sign in an area. Study the terrain on an aerial photo and nail down as best you can the directions from which deer will likely approach your post before or after dark. Then stay out of those travel lanes. Circle a half-mile or so if you need to and enter or exit a stand through barren woods, across an open pasture, etc. Use your head and don't walk down or across deer trails. The fewer deer you bump on the hike in or out, the better the chances that a buck will stay on pattern and walk close to your stand.

> **One day a huge buck sneaks in, sees or smells you in a tree stand and spooks. Now what?**

Sometimes a buck will catch you climbing into or out of a stand. He might look up and see you glassing, rattling or drawing your bow. Yikes, he may circle in downwind and start stamping and blowing. Some days you're just going to get busted!

As badly as you want to keep hunting a buck in your best spot, it's best to leave him alone for a few days, even if you think he didn't get a double nostril of scent. For the next 4 or 5 days, each time a mature deer passes the tree where he busted you, he'll likely scent-check the area. You don't want to be there and get busted again.

Go back and study your aerial maps. Look for a terrain funnel or thick edge somewhere downwind of your first stand. It might be only 50 yards away, or 200 to 400 yards out. Either way, hang another stand and get after the buck again. There's a good chance you'll see him from your fresh setup.

> **One afternoon does and young bucks stroll in to feed beneath your stand or within 50 yards of your ground blind, but a big deer doesn't come until right at dark. Shooting light wanes, and the deer stay there, eating and mingling. You're pinned on post, so what do you do?**

You run into this problem a lot, especially when hunting in and around a crop field early or late in the season. If you climb down from your stand or out of your blind, you'll obviously scare the wits out of a bunch of animals. Pressure like that a couple of nights in a row can cause deer, and especially mature bucks, to change their habits quickly.

One offbeat solution is to have a buddy drive across a field or down an old logging and fetch you from a stand after dark. In most areas these days, whitetails see and hear vehicles all the time. A truck rattling across a field or through the woods will scatter deer, but the animals won't associate that with hunting. And the best thing is that a big buck doesn't see you climb out of a stand or blind. When you leave in the truck, does and sometimes bucks will often pop right back out to feed, especially early in the season. You can usually go back and hunt the feeding area the next afternoon and see the same deer.

You see a Pope & Young buck a few times during archery season, but you can't get a shot at him. Gun season rolls around and an army of hunters hit the woods. How do you bowhunt that big deer now?

For starters, be confident the buck still roams the area. There will be a lot of shooting around, and there's a chance a gun hunter will kill "your" buck. But more likely, the pressure will simply change the deer's pattern and turn him even more nocturnal.

"Stick with it and set your vacation days to coincide with the rut if that is an option," says Ronnie "Cuz" Strickland, an ardent deer hunter and executive producer of Mossy Oak's television shows and videos. "I believe that in a pressure situation there are only a few windows of opportunity to kill a nice buck you've been hunting awhile, and the rut is one of them. Hunt twice as far back in thickets as you did earlier in the season. A hot doe might pull that buck out of cover, but it won't be too far out. You'll generally shoot a big deer with your bow where it's thick and tangled."

You've hunted a spot for years, and have shot your share of does and 100-inch bucks. What can you do to finally score big?

An old saying goes something like, "You can be the best deer hunter in the world, but if you hunt a spot where no big bucks live, you'll never shoot a trophy." So start looking for a new place to hunt. A farm or woodlot 30 to 60 miles down the road from where you've been hunting all those years might have more high-protein feed, better genetics, heavier cover, less pressure … and more good bucks. Get permission and just like that your odds of tagging a trophy animal shoot way up.

Hang around the local bow or gun shop, diner or check station. Chat up other hunters who shoot good bucks. Who knows, maybe they've got an opening in their club. The Internet is a great tool. Visit your state's website and research harvest figures and big-buck data for various counties and public-hunting areas. E-mail a deer biologist for advice on the top spots to hunt a trophy. Keep looking around until you locate a better hunting ground.

You finally get a crack at an enormous buck one day and miss! Now what?

When we mess up, we typically get all agitated and do something drastic, like moving our stand a half-mile or more, or picking up and leaving a spot altogether. "But deer don't necessarily associate a shot with danger," says David Hale of Knight & Hale Game Calls. "When a gun goes off, there is a lot of noise, but a buck, especially if he was 100 yards or farther away, might not have known what happened, or where the shot came from. If you miss with an arrow, don't sweat it. To a buck, that might have been nothing more than a limb breaking or falling. I don't think a big deer pays nearly as much attention to being missed as he does to seeing or smelling you."

If you blow it, chill out, and then fine-tune your setup. "It's probably best to move your stand 50 to 100 yards to another ridge or funnel, or go hunt another stand you already have set up in the area," says Hale. "A buck might return through the area, but he'll probably skirt the spot where you missed him, at least for a few days. But you might get another shot from a new setup."

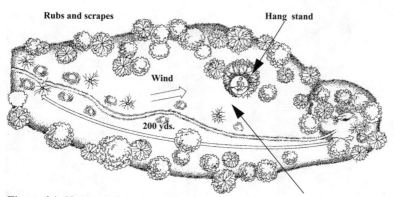

Figure 24. Hunting where a buck's rubs and scrapes begin to peter out on the way to a bedding area can be most effective at first or last light.

Quick Tip: Scout for a spot on the end of a ridge or in the foot of a hollow where a buck's scrapes begin to peter out en route to a thick bedding area. Play the wind, set up there and try to ambush the deer at first or last light. A buck might linger around his "last" scrapes before he beds down at dawn, and they will also be the first scrapes he checks as he prowls forth in late afternoon.

Bow and Gun Dilemmas

Problem: Your bow shoots arrows tipped with field points great, but when you switch to broadheads, they wobble and fly all over the place.

Solution: A broadhead must be perfectly straight on an arrow before it will fly true. Visit a bow shop and have all your hunting arrows and broadheads spin-checked on a machine to make sure they are in alignment. While you're at it, have a pro check and tune your bow, arrow rest, peep, sight, etc. If your bow is just a little out of tune, even perfectly aligned broadheads and shafts won't fly as true as they might.

It takes several range sessions and at least 50 shots to find the most accurate powder/bullet combo for your muzzleloader.

Problem: You're having trouble sighting in your 270 or 30-06 (or any caliber).

Solution: If you can't shoot at least 2-inch groups at 100 yards from a bench with today's excellent factory ammunition, you've likely got a scope-mount problem. Pull the scope and its rings and bases, and reinstall everything. Or better yet, have a pro at your local gun shop do it. Nine times out of 10 this will solve your problem and shrink your groups.

Problem: Your muzzleloader sprays bullets all over a target.

Solution: Muzzleloader technology has come a long way, but blackpowder rifles, and even the popular in-lines, are still finicky. In my experience, it takes two or three range sessions and at least 50 shots to find a powder/bullet combo that will group 2 inches at 100 yards out of any 50-caliber gun. Test various powder charges and at least three different saboted bullets in the 200- to 300-grain range. You can shoot 150 grains of Pyrodex in one of today's magnum muzzleloaders, but some rifles shoot more accurately with 100 grains. Use the hassle-free, 50-grain pellets. Start shooting at 50 yards, and gradually work your way out to 100 yards sighting bullets to hit one to two inches high. With a finely tuned 50-caliber in-line, any hunter should be able to kill a buck out to 150 yards.

Chapter 15

Western Whitetails

On a map of the United States, visualize where the contiguous Eastern woodlands end west of the Mississippi River. Now park your finger in the Texas Panhandle, drive it west to the Continental Divide and turn north to Montana. You've just traced a big chunk of the Great Plains, where the topography runs from grasslands to sage flats to chiseled badlands.

For all its diversity, the country has a couple of common denominators. First, it is vast and open, incredibly so in most places. Second, it is home to stable and rising populations of whitetails, and within those growing herds live lots of trophy bucks. While most hunters still talk about elk and mule deer and the West in one breath, I believe that is about to change. Western whitetail hunting is hot, and getting hotter all the time.

I shot my first plains whitetail in the North Texas Panhandle several years ago. That hunt was so fun I now bow or gun hunt at least once out West each fall.

Open-Country Bucks

Years ago on one of my first trips west, I gazed out the truck window and thought, *Man, this is a far cry from Virginia.* Since deer live mostly in the woods back home, I naturally figured they would live in the timber, sparse as it was, out here, too. While many bucks stay in the oak brush and in the cottonwoods down by the creeks and rivers, a lot of big deer also inhabit sprawling, grassy hills and canyons.

Out in a place like western Kansas or eastern Colorado, deer feel relatively safe out in the open, where they can see well in all directions. It took me awhile to figure it out, but now I know that plains whitetails rely on their eyes more than their noses to detect potential danger.

If you hunt back East or in the South, you won't see mature bucks in the open very much, unless they're feeding or trailing a doe to a field or clearing early or late in the day. Out on the plains, though, you might glass a 170-class "hawg" bedded out in the low grass of a 5000-acre pasture. It's pretty wild. One of the main things to remember is that it doesn't take much cover to hide a big deer out West.

Seeing is Believing

If you think about it, hunting whitetails is as simple as one, two, three. One, evaluate the habitat. Two, narrow down the deer-activity zones. Three, pattern the bucks that roam those zones.

You can't hunt effectively out West without top-quality optics.

On the plains you do all that with long-range observation. Since you can sit on a wind-swept ridge in eastern Wyoming or Montana and seemingly see from one end of the state to the other, a set of $800 to $1,000 Leica, Swarovski or Zeiss binoculars is not just a luxury, but a necessity.

You need to then focus on a couple of things. First, many of the linear river and creek bottoms that cut the plains hold some type of agricultural crop like alfalfa or wheat. Glass fields at dawn and dusk, and you will see deer and often a mother lode of animals.

One October some buddies and I flew to Montana, drove 5 hours east of the Great Falls airport and pulled into our hunting ranch at sundown. Talk about good timing! We stopped at the first kelly-green alfalfa field we came to, pulled a king's ransom of binoculars and spotting scopes from our duffels and glassed 30 racked

The timber, brush and browse along Montana's Milk River are nirvana for whitetails. Bucks feed in alfalfa fields close by and grow huge racks. It's awesome habitat and one of my favorite spots to bow hunt.

bucks feeding and sniffing too many does to count. Now that's what I call narrowing the plains and finding deer in a hurry.

Next, examine the cuts, coulees, brushy draws and strips of timber that rim the fields and twist back into the grasslands, sage flats or thin timber along a river. These are the travel corridors for deer, and most of them are filled with chokecherries, buffalo berries, a variety of mast and other secondary food sources.

Anytime I'm in big country for a week, I like to spend at least two days scouting from ridges with a binocular and a spotting scope. If the rifle season is open, I carry my 270 or 30-06 and lay it beside me as I work. I'll bust a buck if the opportunity arises, but mostly I try to pattern the whitetails. This type of low-impact looking is especially vital when you're trying to find a little cover strip or funnel in which to set up and archery hunt a big deer in the wide-open spaces.

At dawn, I glass does and bucks leaving fields and walking the draws and timber strips back to their beds. In the afternoons, I watch where the first deer pop out of the cover and into a feeding area. Of course the best-case scenario, and a feasible one in many areas, is to see a couple of 8- or 10-pointers in the 130- to 160-inch class cruising into or out of a field in the same spot 2 or 3 days in a row.

Try to reference the bucks' entry and exit routes on an aerial photo. Then one day around lunchtime sneak to the edge of a field, analyze the trails, rubs and scrapes you are sure to find in the bordering cover, and hang a tree stand or set a ground blind for an ambush. It's an easy, simple strategy, and it works.

Stalking Bucks

One December in the Texas Panhandle I sat on a hillside at dawn and glassed a buck that left a wheat field and walked a mile up a winding draw, his rack glittering all the way in the rising sun. Just like that, the antlers disappeared! I glassed the surrounding terrain for 15 minutes before deciding that the buck had bedded down for the day. Then the fun began.

This sure doesn't look like whitetail habitat, but I glassed a lot of fine bucks in the fertile river drainage below.

At first glance, the grassy plains look big, open and flat. But once you get to hiking around, you find that the country is all carved up and perfect for stalking. I hiked for an hour, ducking behind ridges and points and hustling down draws and dry creek washes. I duck-walked through saddles and other low spots. I played the wind, but I paid more attention to using the terrain and staying out of sight and mind of deer. As I said earlier, in open country, bucks use their eyes more than noses and ears to detect danger.

> **Quick tip:** As I mentioned in Chapter 1, whitetails from Texas to Montana don't seem to wind you and stamp and blow as much as they do in the Midwest, South or East. My theory is that deer cannot pick up human scent as well or as far in arid regions where the humidity is low. Does this mean you don't have to play the wind out West? No, but I find you can cheat the breeze a little bit, especially if you wear a scent-control suit and spray your clothes, pack and other gear with an odor neutralizer. Just don't move around too much on stand, or skyline on a ridge when still-hunting or stalking. Remember, plains bucks are sharp-eyed devils. They'll spot you from hundreds of yards away and bolt.

I belly-crawled up a rocky ridge and eased in behind some oak brush. Where was the buck? I looked for 20 minutes before I caught the twinkle of sunlight on a polished tine. The key to glassing the plains is to look long, hard and *low* in the grass or sage to find a piece of a buck. Once you do, the whole animal will pop into focus.

As luck would have it, the deer was bedded 150 yards away and slightly below me. My first thought was to get my rifle ready and then throw a rock or yell at the deer. I'd done that a couple of times before and busted bucks when they stood up to see what the heck was going on. But what if the deer flew up and busted out across the prairie? I'd have one of those fast, wild off-hand shots. I'd also missed a couple of bucks that way.

I thought better of it and crawled 10 yards left and then 20 yards back to the right. Finally I found a small hole in the brush. I centered the scope's crosshair on the point of the bedded deer's shoulder and gently, oh-so-gently, touched off the shot.

I hiked off the ridge and climbed the knoll. I knelt with the buck and grasped his antlers. From the little hill where he had bedded, you could see for miles and there wasn't a tree in sight. It was a fitting end to another cool plains hunt.

Western Gear

Rifles: Since you might have to stretch a shot at a buck out to 300 yards or so, carry a flat-shooter chambered for 270, 280, 30-06 or 7mm Magnum. Top it with a quality variable-power scope. For my money, you can't beat the venerable Leupold Vari-X. Sight a premium 130- to 165-grain bullet to hit $1\frac{1}{2}$ to 2 inches high at 100 yards, which will put you pretty much dead on at 200 yards and only 6 inches or so low at 300. Attach a Harris Bipod to your rifle, or use a set of Stony Point shooting sticks.

Optics: You'll glass immense country for hours with heat mirage. As mentioned, you can't do that effectively without a top-quality binocular. I use a full-size 10x Leica Trinovid, one of the best optics in the world, along with a 15x-45x spotting scope to size up the bodies and racks of bucks. My choice is Leupold's Wind River spotting scope, which is a great optic for the money.

Tree Stands: Tall, straight, limbless trees are rare in many parts of the West, so most of the time you can forget about using a climber. But you can bow or gun hunt from a fixed-position or ladder perch hung in a big cottonwood or a stunted, scrubby tree.

Ground Blinds: My favorite is a natural one. Play the wind and set up against a huge, round bale of alfalfa or hay in a field. Or cut a few cedars and build a little hide. You might try a portable camouflage blind

with a roof and plenty of shooting holes. Be sure to tuck the blind in shade or cover along a fencerow or in a copse of grass or

In the open spaces out West, blow a high-volume grunt call and rattle a big set of horns.

Modern Gear Tip: If you're not using a laser rangefinder, you're hunting in the dark ages. A high-tech laser tells you *precisely* how far away a buck is—22 yards, 122, 268, whatever—and it gives you the confidence you need to make the shot. The large and pricey Leica Geovid, which features a superb 7x binocular, is my favorite for rifle hunting in the big, open West. For bowhunting anywhere in the country, I use a compact laser from Leica, Nikon or Bushnell.

trees, and brush it up with natural vegetation. Any ground blind, natural or portable, should be well hidden, or it will spook deer. That's the case not only out West but also anywhere across the country.

Calls: The country is big and the wind blows almost all the time—two reasons to carry a loud grunt tube, like Knight & Hale's EZ Grunter or Primos' Magnum call. Bang a large set of rattling horns during the mid-November rut to reach out and strike a buck.

Decoys: A fake buck or doe can work great out West because deer can see it from a long way off. Stake a decoy along the edge of a grain field in the afternoon, or, better yet in my experience, back in a grassy draw or river bottom on a morning hunt. Decoys work best from late in the pre-rut through the mid-November breeding season. As mentioned in Chapter 6, a fake doe or buck will sometimes spook deer, especially when the animals get close to your imposter. If you see deer flaring from your decoy, take it down.

If you're not using a laser range finder, you're hunting in the dark ages. The optic reveals precise yardage to a buck and gives you the confidence to make the shot.

Rifle-Shooting Pointers

- Think out a shot before it happens. Say you're hiking along a ridge in Wyoming. Look down into an adjacent coulee and wonder, *What would I do if a big buck jumped out of there? Where would he run? Could I use that sage bush up ahead for a rest? Is it 150 or 250 yards across the canyon?* That kind of mental preparation helps a lot when a buck does jump up.

I use either a Harris bipod or a set of Stony Point shooting sticks when rifle hunting out West. With a solid rest, I feel comfortable shooting at a buck 300 yards away. Any farther and I stalk closer.

- On plains and prairies, your biggest challenge is judging distance. Is a buck 175 or 275 yards away? It can be tough to tell, especially if you've been hunting the thick woods back East or South all your life. Pinpoint the yardage to a whitetail with your laser range finder.
- When hiking along, set your riflescope at 4x or 6x. If you jump a buck, he'll be relatively easy to pick up in the wide field of view. When setting up a long-range shot, you should have plenty of time to crank the scope's magnification to 7x or 9x if you need to. Be sure to turn the magnification back down when you go back to still-hunting.

- When setting up a shot at a buck, go prone and lay your rifle over your daypack. Or sit or kneel and pin a rifle's fore-end (the stock, never the barrel) against the side of a tree or fence post. A bipod or shooting sticks work great if you can set them up quickly and easily. A buck can get away though if you spend too much time fooling around with a portable rest. Before a hunt out West, practice flipping down a bipod or setting up sticks so you'll be ready.

- Don't worry too much about the uphill/downhill thing. When a shooting angle is less than 45 degrees, and most of the time it is, hold dead on a deer's lungs and touch off the shot.

- It might be calm where you're sitting and glassing, but the wind might be gusting out where a buck feeds or noses a doe 150 to 300 yards away. Glass the leaves, grass or brush around a buck. If the wind blows only 5 to 10 mph or so, hold dead-on the animal. But if the leaves or brush shake and whip, you'll need to hold your scope's crosshair slightly into the wind on shots past 100 yards.

- When a buck is broadside, aim for the middle of the dark crease behind the shoulder. If the bullet hits within 6 inches of your point of aim, you will kill the deer cleanly every time. If a buck is quartering on, aim for the point of the shoulder facing you. When a deer is quartering away, move your aim slightly back on the ribs, and align the crosshair on the offside front leg. Years ago, many hunters took neck shots, but they are taboo these days, and that is the way it should be. A neck shot is too risky, even at close range.

Chapter 16

Canada's Monster Whitetails

When you spend thousands of dollars and travel thousands of miles to hunt new country, you go with an odd blend of anticipation and trepidation. Will I like the people? Will I see a lot of deer? Will I get a crack at the buck of my dreams? Can I handle it if I do?

Thus I arrived one November day at Ministikwan Lodge, a ring of clapboard cabins tucked deep in the bush of west-central Saskatchewan, hard on the shores of the lake that bears its name. Walking around and checking out the place, I imagined it to be a paradise for bear hunters and pike fishermen. But were there any whitetails around?

"C'mon in, I want to show you something." Bruce Bazelinski appeared big as a bear in the doorway of the dining hall, but his voice was surprisingly soft and soothing. I followed the outfitter into the room. He waved a thick hand at the deer heads on the wall and said, "Whaddya think, will you Americans come up here to hunt bucks like that?"

My jaw dropped. All the deer, which had been shot by resident hunters just miles from the lodge, easily scored Boone & Crockett. One, the freakish, No. 6 all-time Saskatchewan non-typical, really caught my eye. The gnarly buck had the most impressive rack I had ever seen. We swilled coffee and chatted, and then Bazelinski showed me to my sleeping cabin. With visions of those mounts in my head, I prepped my gear for a week of hunting. I didn't sleep a wink that night.

The air in the timber on opening morning was black, still and way too warm. The temperature hovered in the 40s, unheard of for mid-November in western Canada. I sweated on the walk into my blind and sat chilling as the sun came up, pink as salmon flesh in the east. I shivered and conjured a thought of an old buck easing through the willows and spruce, hips swaying, a rack the size of a kid's rocking chair on his

Every Saskatchewan buck has lots of character. This symmetrical 8-pointer had flat, almost palmated, tines. The deer was not the heaviest I have shot up North, but it still weighed 300 pounds!

thick head. I peeked over at Grant Morton; he, too, seemed deep in thought. I liked my guide, a soft-spoken fellow with a head of silver hair and a wonderful sense of humor. The first time I met him and shook his hand, Grant said in his thick Canadian accent, "I'm a moose hunter. You're the deer guy, so hunt any way you want to. I'll show you good spots and help if I can, eh?"

Dawn came and went. We didn't see a deer, but that is not uncommon in the North Country. One of the first things you learn is that you won't see a buck every day that you go hunting in Saskatchewan.

Back at the lodge over lunch, the talk naturally turned to big whitetails and the weather. The heat wave was rare for this country, which in a normal winter has bone-chilling temperatures in the single digits and 30 or more inches of snow. On opening day, the mercury had soared into the 50s.

"Our deer would normally be rutting by now, but this heat has them shut down, eh?" said Bazelinski, who seemed to question himself as he spoke, something I find intriguing about the Canadians. "But the big bucks are lying tight in the bush and only coming out for a few minutes at dawn and dusk, eh?"

We put out heads together and decided my best shot would be to scout fields and edges for fresh tracks and other sign. Then I would take a ground stand and hope for the best at first and last light. Even then it would take a lot of luck to be in the right place at the right time in this big country. But isn't that deer hunting anywhere?

For the next 5 days I hunted in the heat and saw some deer, but no shooter bucks. On the last morning I found what I was looking for: A line of huge scrapes pawed on the edge of a pasture, rimmed by poplar rubs as thick as my thigh. At least one mature buck had started rutting, and I was going to spend my last afternoon looking for him.

I eased out into the field about 2 P.M. My plan was to build a little hide of hay bales 200 yards or so off the scrapes. I would sit, wait and hope the buck, or one of his rivals, would stick his neck out. I reckoned that in this heat it wouldn't happen for at least a couple of hours, if it happened at all, so I ambled along out in the open. But wait! Two does were already out in the field, nosing for forbs in broad daylight. I pitched to the ground and crawled to the nearest bale.

For 2 hours I watched does stream out into the field. At one point I counted 30 animals, but then lost track as they mingled in and out of my binoculars. Considering I had seen only a handful of deer the first 6 days, it was odd, but things can change that fast if you keep a positive attitude and keep hunting hard on the cusp of the rut.

My first Saskatchewan 10-pointer scored nearly 170 and weighed 315 pounds. Awesome!

The antics of one of the larger does, she must have weighed more than 200 pounds, caught my eye. Obviously annoyed, she ran from her fawns, turning back to kick them away. She was on the brink of estrus! Surely at least one good buck should be lurking around. I glassed harder than ever, moving my hands slowly with so many sharp eyes in front of me. Darkness was coming on fast, bringing its chill and metallic light, when all hell broke loose.

A buck thundered out of the birch and into the field. I didn't have to look twice. It was a nice 8-pointer, a 130-incher I would gladly have shot back home in Virginia, but he was not the buck I came to Canada to kill. He ran at the doe and, with the moves of a cutting horse, corralled her. The animals ran round and round, flashing out of sight and then curling back. I spun on my elbows, looking wildly. The deer galloped back, and this time there were three of them!

A huge buck ran alongside the 8-pointer and flicked him aside, then went after the doe, grunting like a market hog. They circled round and round, at one point closing to within 60 yards of my bale. I figured that was my chance. I rose to my knees, swung my 30-06, found the blur of the buck in the scope, and fired. The shot shattered the silence, but I didn't hear the reassuring "whump" of the bullet. Frantically, I bolted the rifle and looked deep into the growing shadows. There, the buck had pulled up in a swale! I centered the crosshair on his shoulder and fired again.

Strange how it happens like that. For days, you don't see much. Then one minute a giant buck gallops into your life. I walked over and sat with the deer awhile. I dug my hands into his thick winter coat and watched my knuckles disappear. No wonder the buck hated to move in the heat, but the rut had brought him out into the open. I twisted his head into my lap and ran my fingers over the dark tines, 10 of them long and heavy. The G-2 on the right side had three cheaters, giving the rack even more character.

Grant had heard the shots. He drove up and jumped out of his truck, anxious as a cat. He saw the buck in the headlights and grinned. We gave each other a bear hug and a big clap on the back. "Now how shall we load this beast?" he asked. "He will weigh a good 300 pounds."

Somehow we managed. We rode back to camp, chattering as only hunters can, savoring every detail of the day, sharing the moment.

We scored the rack that night in the outfitter's garage. The main-framed 10-pointer taped 168 inches, and we guessed him to be 5 ½ or 6 ½ years old.

Skinning the buck, I found that the first 165-grain boattail had clipped the buck's lungs, so the second shot had been unnecessary. But you don't take any chances when the buck of your dreams is still standing and prone to run off.

On the ride back to the airport the next day, I reflected on the hunt. The room and board at Ministikwan had been Spartan but plenty good enough for deer camp. Grant Morton had been a great guide and even better company. I had killed my biggest buck ever, quite a feat considering the heat wave and the lack of snow. I sat there and thought as I gazed out at the passing bush, *No wonder this place is fast becoming a deer hunter's paradise.*

Perspectives on Canada

That hunt occurred way back in November 1987, when Saskatchewan was just opening its doors to American hunters. I was one of the first hunting writers to travel up there and kill a giant buck. The story I wrote about it for the National Rifle Association's *American Hunter* magazine generated more than 3000 letters and phone calls for the outfitter, who booked his lodge full for years to come. The pilgrimage of Americans heading north for trophy bucks had begun.

Today, of course, Saskatchewan is legendary for its big whitetails. The biggest of all is the current world-record typical shot by Saskatchewan farmer Milo Hanson near the town of Biggar in November 1993. That unbelievably symmetrical 12-pointer scored 213-1/8 Boone and Crockett points. Someday in the not-so-distant future, I believe a lucky hunter will break that record. It might be in Iowa or Kansas. Or the record might just as well stay home in Saskatchewan.

I certainly don't expect to shoot the new No. 1 deer, but I'll keep going back to Saskatchewan every chance I get. The potential of the country ... the heavy, gnarly bucks ... the remoteness of the bush ... I love it all. It is a truly unique experience, and I encourage every serious deer hunter to partake of it at least once in his or her life. If and when you go, here are some things to expect.

You'll be surprised—no, make that shocked—the first time you travel to west-central Saskatchewan and the provincial forest where most of the nonresident hunting now occurs. There are no rolling hardwood ridges, no river or creek bottoms, no food plots or cornfields like you're used to hunting back home. All you'll find at the end of a 3-hour drive north from the Saskatoon airport is hundreds of square miles of willow, birch, spruce, pine and balsam fir bordered by hundreds of square miles of muskeg, sloughs and lakes. The bush looks like a great place to hunt for moose and black bears. But whitetails? You start to wonder. But believe me, the giant deer are there.

You'll be shocked at how dark it is the first morning you step into the bush, even during a full moon, and even when the Northern Lights dance green and blue in the sky. You cannot see your boots or even the rifle in your hands as you sneak toward your blind. Except perhaps for the howling of wolves a mile away, it will be quiet, eerily quiet. No songbirds flit about, and no squirrels scamper around at sunrise. Only silence pounds in the dank timber.

In a normal November, you'll be shocked at how cold it is. Snow will cover the ground, and the mercury will hover in the single digits or teens ... on days when it gets above zero. Bundled up like the Michelin Man, rubbing hand warmers and wiggling your toes in your boots, you'll shiver in a blind from sunup till sundown. You'll think, *I never knew it could get this cold.* Ah, but what stokes you to keep hunting is the realization that the colder it is, the better the big deer move.

Most of all, you'll be shocked at how few deer you see. You can hunt for a week and spot maybe a couple dozen whitetails around feeding areas and in travel funnels. Some days, you might spot only one or two deer, but one of those animals might carry a rack that scores 150 inches …180 inches …or more! And that is why you travel thousands of miles to hunt the cold, dank bush. There is a good chance you'll shoot a good buck. There is a slim chance you'll kill a Boone & Crocket. There is a miniscule chance you'll tag the next world-record.

This beast had thick mass and 10 black tines. Note the third main beam that corkscrews out over his nose. I told you these bucks had character!

That thought, ridiculous as it may sound, lingered in my mind on a recent hunt in the North Country, even though I'd spotted exactly four deer in two days of dawn-till-dusk hunting. But there was always tomorrow. A 150-, a 180-, a 200-inch buck was out there, feeding or scraping or nosing a doe. He was out there. Thinking like that kept me going.

On the third day I spotted one deer, a fat doe. Lunchtime came and went. The silence pounded on. I had plenty of time to think about all the things going on in my life. I read a book, peeking up every once in a while to scan the spruce for a flash of hide or an antler. I waited.

You'll be shocked at how fast things happen in the bush. It's amazing how those big deer just show up out front of your blind. Around 4:00

Quick Tip: In the aftermath of 9-11, don't even think about traveling to Canada with a hunting rifle unless you have the proper documentation. You can get by with a driver's license, but a passport is much better. You'll also need to complete a Nonresident Firearms Declaration Form, which is available at the border and at various Canadian Internet sites. If your paperwork is in order, you should have little trouble breezing through customs at the Edmonton or Saskatoon airport. Security officials there are used to screening many American deer hunters each fall.

that afternoon, a twig popped 100 yards to my left. It sounded like a cherry bomb going off in the stillness. I snapped to attention and heard a deer stamp its foot and blow aggressively. It had to be a rutting buck! Hide flashed in the spruce trees. The deer trotted past my blind, muscles rippling and rack riding high, tines and points all over the place. My 270 roared.

You'll be shocked when you lay your hands on your first Saskatchewan whitetail. This buck had a bull-thick chest and a neck that had begun to swell for the rut. No lie, he weighed 320 pounds. I sunk my knuckles deep into his coarse hide. I grabbed his mocha-colored rack. It was non-typical, with 13 points, a 12-inch double main beam and a 6-inch drop tine. The deer was not Boone and Crockett, but he was the kind of beast you go up there to hunt.

Hunting Times and Methods

In my experience, the best time to book a deer hunt in Saskatchewan, or in neighboring Manitoba or Alberta for that matter, is around November 20. Thanksgiving week is generally hot. That is when the rut peaks, and the big deer come out of the spruce woodwork to troll for does or chase them. You can get lucky with a bow or a muzzleloader in October or early November. You can also sit for days, as I have many times, without spotting a shooter.

I look at it this way. If you are going to spend thousands of hard-earned dollars on a dream hunt to Canada, and if you can swing it only once in your life, you might as well go when the conditions are right and the big bucks go on the prowl. That is always during the rifle season in mid to late November. Hunt one of the prime weeks, and four or five guys in camp will typically haul in mega bucks that score from 140 to 170 inches or more. One of those guys might be you.

Rut hunts with the best outfitters in western Canada fill up quickly, so book your trip early. You might have to plan a hunt a year or two down the road, but that is all right. Don't let an outfitter talk you in to hunting a week in late October or early November, when he has openings. Wait and go in late November when the big deer get active. I can't emphasize that point enough.

We use ground blinds when filming Saskatchewan hunts. During the November rut, we sit in the huts from sunrise to dark. You never know when a monster will gallivant by.

As I've alluded to several times, most of the hunting in Saskatchewan is from ground blinds, or from box blinds set 10 feet or so off the ground. Some outfitters utilize tree stands if it's not too darn cold in November.

Whether you hunt from a stand or blind, a good Canadian guide will encourage you to sit all day long near a food source or high-interaction travel area. He'll show you to a stand in the dark, and come back to get you after dark each evening. Most Americans are not used to sitting in

> **Modern Outfitter Tip:** All American deer hunters must hire an outfitter in Canada. I've hunted with many Saskatchewan guides over the years, and none better than Grant Kuypers of Buck Paradise Outfitters (www.buckparadise.com; 306-344-4638). Kuypers hunts two huge concessions in west-central Saskatchewan, and each area has lots of big deer. The food, accommodations and guides at Buck Paradise are first rate. I believe Kuypers will be one of the premier whitetail outfitters in Saskatchewan for years to come.

one spot for 8 to 10 hours, and it is admittedly tough. But if you want to kill a big northern deer, it is the thing to do.

One day I sat shivering in a ground blind and didn't see an animal until 2:30 P.M. The first and only deer I spotted was a 155-inch buck, and I killed him. Another day in Saskatchewan, a 148-inch buck nosed a doe past my ground blind at 9:30 A.M. You just never know when the rut is on, especially if the moon is full during a November hunt. Suck it up and sit all day in the land of the giants. There's a good chance you'll shoot your dream buck.

Grant Kuypers (left) put me on this heavy-horned brute. Kuypers is one of the best Canadian outfitters I've ever hunted with.

North Country Gear

- **Clothes:** Wear sweat-wicking thermal underwear and top it off with layers of chamois or fleece. Wear Gore-Tex outwear to repel the snow and knock off the bone-chilling wind. Top-quality gloves and socks are a must. In short, be prepared to hunt the coldest temperatures you can imagine. If it is unusually warm on your hunt in November, in the 30s or 40s, you can always strip off layers.
- **Whites:** Canadian law requires hunters to wear white (or orange or red) head to toe during rifle season. Cabela's sells a nice suit of fleece whites.
- **Boots:** Wear rubber-bottom "pacs" rated to at least minus 40.
- **Optics:** As mentioned throughout this book, you can't shoot a big buck you can't see. Don't even think about going on a dream hunt without a quality riflescope and binocular. Most shots at big deer in the thick bush are short, but you might hunt an open ridge, swamp or clearing area where you can see 200 to 400 yards or farther. Carry your laser rangefinder.
- **Rifles and loads:** These are the largest deer you'll ever hunt. A mature buck can weigh a legitimate 300 pounds or more, but you don't need to be overgunned. In fact, most hunters shoot a 270 or 30-06 more accurately than they do a shoulder-thumping 300 or 338 Winchester Mag. For north-country bucks, I use either a 270 with a 130-grain Trophy Bonded Bear Claw bullet, or a 30-06 with a 150- or 165-grain bullet. In short, the rifle/load combo you use for whitetails back home will be fine.
- **Odds and ends:** Carry plenty of disposable hand and toe warmers (the kind you shake and chemically activate). Two or three paperback thrillers will help pass all those hours in a blind. Since you'll be out alone all day in the remote bush, pack along some basic survival gear such as a compass, waterproof matches, water and a compact first-aid kit.

Chapter 17

Practical Deer Management

Managing whitetails on private lands was born down in Texas and other southern states years ago. At warp speed, it has zoomed into a booming business across the U.S. Lodges, outfitters, hunt clubs and large landowners shell out millions each year to plant, lime and fertilize food plots. Many hunters/managers supplement with high-protein feed and mineral licks. Some of the really high-dollar operations build high fences to keep in all the huge bucks they grow.

Terry Drury shot this big buck coming to a Bio-Logic plot.

It has been a great trend, and it is improving the health of herds and producing thick-bodied, big-racked deer from Alabama to Iowa to New York. But sometimes lost in all the hoopla is the fact that many of today's whitetail hunters don't have the funds, time, equipment or access to the acres needed to implement a full-blown management program.

So what's in it for us little guys? Can we attract deer and possibly increase the body weight and rack size of bucks on the 50- to 500–acre farms and woodlots we typically hunt? Can we micromanage whitetails with minimal time and effort, and without breaking the bank?

"There's no question you can," says Jim Crumley, a guy who speaks from experience.

Crumley, who created Trebark Camouflage in 1980 and merged his company with Mossy Oak a few years ago, once purchased 66 acres in southwestern Virginia. Though the tract was very small, it featured a nice mix of openings, woods and cover for whitetails. "That place had 20 acres of old pasture and 20 acres of cedar trees," notes Crumley. "The rest was mature oak forest. For management purposes, you need to start out with a place that has good habitat, regardless of the size. Ideally, I believe that's one-third fields surrounded by woods and thickets. You can plant the fields to attract deer. The hardwoods offer acorns and other natural foods. The thickets provide browse and bedding and hiding spots for the animals."

Back in those days, Crumley didn't own any farm equipment. "I hired a man to come in and bush-hog 30-by-50-yard strips through the old pasture," he says. "I didn't do any expensive or time-consuming clearing or tilling for food plots. I simply had the guy drag a rock rake over the mowed strips to break the ground, and then I seeded some clover and perennial rye grass in September."

The results were impressive, and proof that you can attract deer *the first season* you implement a habitat-enhancement plan, even on a small tract. "By the second week of October, when bow season opened, lush, green clover was coming up in the strips," recalls Crumley. "Lots of deer were coming to it from everywhere."

For the next couple of years Crumley improved the habitat in other simple but functional ways. For example, he pruned trees to increase browse and fertilized native forage like honeysuckle and blackberries. But the cornerstone of his management program continued to be those food strips.

"Another good thing about planting clover and perennial ryegrass is that you can simply hire someone to come in and bush-hog the strips at the end of the summer," he says. "The plants will reseed themselves. If deer hit the clover really hard, you might have to reseed it every other year, but most of the time you can just fertilize the strips twice a year, spring and fall, and you're in business for a while."

Crumley sold the 66 acres in the early 1990s. He now manages whitetails on a larger tract he owns on the banks of Virginia's James River, but that's another story. Thinking back, the camo guru and die-hard bowhunter figures he spent $500 the first year to get his management plan off the ground. The next 2 years, the bush hogging and fertilizing costs were minimal. Even factoring in inflation, most hunters can handle an expense like that, especially if two or three guys pitch in and split the bill.

Was his investment worth it? "The first season I managed the property, morning hunts were tough," says Crumley. "But in the evenings you could set up off the food strips, in cover toward bedding areas, and have lots of bowshots at does and young bucks. By the second and third seasons I saw noticeably more deer, and the quality of the bucks improved some. No doubt, I got my money's worth on those 66 acres."

That is precisely the point I want to make. You don't have to be a huge landowner or a millionaire to manage deer. Just team up with a few buddies, pool your funds and put in some elbow grease and sweat over the spring and summer. Micromanage your small or mid-size tract for healthier whitetails, more good bucks and a better hunting experience now and into the future.

Food-Plot Primer

Unless you've been living in a cave for the last few years, you've heard about food plots and their many benefits for whitetails. Well, if you can swing the bucks, you ought to get into the game and plant a few fields on any property you own or lease. Along with food strips, plots will help you attract and hold more does and bucks. Dr. Grant Woods, one of the world's top whitetail biologists and habitat-improvement specialists, offers some great advice to get you started.

Noted whitetail biologist Dr. Grant Woods swears by Bio-Logic. "The plants in my Bio-Logic plots across the country average 34 percent crude protein," he says. Bucks use that protein to grow heavy bodies and big racks.

- If you hunt a 200- to 400-acre tract, will planting a few food plots keep deer on it all the time? "Probably not," notes Woods. "But food plots can help you go from 50/50 (deer on your property/off it) to 80/20 or maybe even 90/10. For the small landowner or hunt club, decreasing the home range of whitetails is the biggest benefit of food plots."
- The number of plots you should plant depends on the deer density in your area. If you've got, say, five to 10 deer per square mile, one plot every 150 acres or so should do. "But if you planted just one plot on a small piece of land down in South Carolina or a similar state where deer numbers are very high these days, the animals would eat it up in no time," notes Woods. A good average is one plot for every 150 to 200 acres, but again it depends on an area's deer density. Check with a local biologist for deer numbers in your area, and then plant plots according to his recommendations.
- A small landowner or club can get by nicely with micro food plots. "Actually, planting a half-acre plot back in the woods and near cover is a great way for the average person to create a great hidey-hole to hunt," says Woods. The good doctor recommends seeding such a small plot in the fall, after a rain and a few weeks before bow season. Deer will find the plot and lock into a pattern to and from it, but the animals won't have enough time to eat up all the plants. "The biggest plot I would ever plant would probably be 8 acres," points out Woods. "That's huge." Any size in between might do. But again, the size of a plot varies according to an area's deer density.
- "You've got to remember that seeds are living organisms," says woods. "Plant them where they will get enough moisture to germinate. If you live in a fairly dry region, say eastern Kentucky or north Georgia, you'd want to avoid ridge tops. It's too dry up there. Generally speaking, the northeast corner of a slope has the moistest soil, so that would be a good spot for a plot."
- Try to plant a food plot so that it runs north to south, not east to west. Woods notes that a north-south plot provides enough sunlight to grow plants, but there's also plenty of shade. An east-west plot would bake in the sun.
- You can plant a food plot in either spring or fall, depending on your mission. A spring plot provides the most nutrition for deer. Lactating does and bucks growing racks really suck up minerals and nutrients, and they get those from spring plots. You plant a fall plot mostly to attract deer, and to provide the animals with high-quality food into the critical winter months.

Don't disc too deeply! Dr. Grant Woods says never plant seeds more than an inch deep. A quarter to half an inch is about right.

- Sow a spring plot when daytime temperatures reach the 70s or higher, which means the soil temperature will be in the 60s. "You might plant a plot in Florida in late March, or in late April or early May in New York or Pennsylvania," says Woods. "You can plant a plot anywhere into early June as long as you have enough moisture." Plant a fall plot in late summer, but make sure there is enough soil moisture for the seeds to germinate.
- Before planting, a soil test is critical. You need to know the quality of the dirt you're dealing with, and its acidity. Take a small soil sample to your county extension agent; he or she will send it off to a university to get it tested. Cost: about $10.

Try to broadcast seeds over a tilled seedbed just before a light to moderate rain.

- One of the biggest mistakes hunters make is to plant seeds too deep. "You can't go in with a disc and plant seeds 6 to 7 inches deep," Woods says, noting that it would be tough for the plants to get enough moisture and grow and push up through that much dirt. "I like to broadcast seeds over a worked-up seedbed just before a rain," the biologist says. "The water will help work the seeds down into the soil." The bottom line: Never plant seeds more than an inch deep. A quarter-inch is about right.

- Woods likes to mix things up by planting a plot with 60 percent of a perennial blend and 40 percent of an annual blend. The perennial crop gives deer something green to eat all year, and with proper fertilizing and liming, it should last 3 to 5 years. The annual plants grow quickly in either spring or fall. Woods' research shows that an annual blend tastes better to deer, and it really attracts them.

- Woods highly recommends BioLogic products, like New Zealand Premium Perennial or Clover Plus, which he uses in research projects across North America. "I have never tested a blend that provides an equal amount of digestible/absorbable calcium, phosphorous and other minerals for deer," he says. The biologist goes on to point out that the plants in his BioLogic plots across the country average 34 percent or more crude protein. To grow huge bodies and racks, deer need that protein.

- As plants grow, so will native grasses in a plot. Spray with a chemical that kills the grass but does not harm the plants.

- Growing plants suck nutrients out of the ground. Deer eat the plants and then defecate some 24 times a day, sometimes in a plot but many times in the surrounding woods and thickets. So a plot loses nutrients quickly. Have your county extension agent test the soil annually. Lime and fertilize your food plots and strips according to an agent's recommendations.

Five Simple Rules for Small-Land Management

1. Try to buy or lease a property surrounded by posted lands. This is sometimes an option in a suburban area in the Northeast or Mid-Atlantic, where many small landowners do not permit hunting. With little or no pressure on all sides, you should be able to attract lots of whitetails to the food strips or plots you sow. Also, and this is the kicker, there's less chance the bucks you feed will wander off your property and get shot.

Another great option is to establish what the Quality Deer Management Association (www.qdma.com) calls a "QDM cooperative." Under this plan, you and adjoining landowners team up to implement a deer-management program on the collective acreage in an area. Say, for example, you own or lease 400 acres. Five hundred-, 700-, 1000- and 200-acre tracts surround your ground. If everybody joins the cooperative, you and you neighbors can now manage 2800 acres. The more acres you manage, the better. In a nutshell, if everybody in the cooperative plants food strips and plots, shoots a good number of does and lets 1 ½- and 2 ½-year-old bucks walk, everybody across the 2800 acres will see and shoot more mature bucks in seasons to come. And it won't take long before that happens!

A QDM cooperative is strictly voluntary. It does not entitle the neighbors to hunt your property, nor does it permit you access to their land. It is simply a good way for a group to establish an umbrella program that will improve the health of a whitetail herd and the quality of the hunting over a large area. To me, it is the wave of the future, a feasible and cost-effective way for the majority of America's deer hunters to reap the rewards of management.

Even the small-land deer manager should keep meticulous records. Weigh each doe and buck you shoot, and score the racks for future reference.

2. As you mow and seed fields on a tract, be sure to leave plenty of strips of blackberries, raspberries, honeysuckle and other native vegetation. The more diverse the feed on a property, the better it is for the deer. Fertilize native browse with 10-10-10 each spring.

3. Spring is also the time to fertilize a few oak or apple trees on ridges and in draws where you regularly hunt. Grant Woods and other biologists point out that some does and bucks will walk right past bland mast to get to the larger, sweeter acorns or apples you grow near your stands. A time-release fertilizer that gradually feeds trees throughout the year works best. Try BioLogic's Tree-Paks.

4. As you mow or clear ground for food plots, leave strips and pockets of pines or cedars. The trees will offer deer shade in the summer, windbreaks in the winter and travel cover year-round. It's also a good idea to establish a 30- to 50-acre bedding/security sanctuary on a property. You might cut down trash trees and leave them lay. Or simply let a field, power-line or cutover grow up with brush and briars. A sanctuary helps to hold deer on your property, and it will be a safe haven for does and bucks fleeing pressure on surrounding lands.

Never hunt in your sanctuary, but on the fringes of it.

5. Whether you manage 50, 200 or 2000 acres, focus on shooting enough does to help balance the sex ratio of a herd. Let the young bucks walk. If you and your buddies and neighbors keep shooting 1 ½-

Whether you manage 50 or 500 acres, shoot a reasonable number of does and let the young bucks walk.

and 2 ½ -year-old bucks, you'll never grow big deer consistently in your area.

Modern Gear Tip: BioLogic's PH Fertilizer allows you to fertilize and lime a food plot or strip at the same time, saving you hours and money. The 10-10-10 fertilizer has finely ground lime as its filler. Make one pass with the stuff over a plot or strip in spring or fall. It will provide the minerals needed to grow lush plants, and the lime will improve the pH of the soil. For information on PH Fertilizer and the complete line of BioLogic deer-management products, call 1-86-Mossy Oak, or go online at www.mossyoakbiologic.com.

The one big bugaboo in harvesting does is that you'll make some mistakes and shoot button bucks on occasion. To keep that to a minimum, never shoot at a lone deer at long range, or in low light. There's a 50-50 chance that "antlerless" deer will be a buck fawn. Before shooting, study a deer's head with your binoculars. Look for the "knots" of growing antlers on a buck's flat head. A doe fawn's head will appear rounder. It's generally best to wait for a family group of does and fawns to walk out into a green field close to your tree stand. The mature does will be the noticeably larger animals in the pack.

The Modern Mineral Lick

You can take the old salt-lick trick to a new level by using a modern attractant like BioLogic's Whitetail Addiction. Available in liquid, powder or block form, the product combines the proven and powerful draw of sodium with vitamins and minerals that provide deer with nutrients. Some scientists believe that in areas with quality, high-protein feed for deer, the vitamins and minerals supplied by a lick can only help improve the health of deer and the growth of racks. That would make sense, since several studies have shown that deer use mineral licks heavily in spring and summer.

Whitetail Addiction works best in an area with heavy soils, which tend to hold the minerals and keep them active for long periods. Pick a secluded, shady spot and remove leaves and vegetation in a 3- to 6-foot circle. Dump in Whitetail Addiction or set out a block. To keep deer coming back and expanding the site into a huge wallow, refresh with Addiction once or twice a year.

Biologists point out that one mineral lick for every 100 to 200 acres is about right. In addition to food strips and plots, fertilized browse and mast, and pockets of thick cover, a lick is part of a plan that can help you attract and hold deer on a small tract year-round.

You need to know this: Hunting over a salt or mineral lick in the fall is considered baiting and illegal in some states. Check your regulations!

Team up with a few buddies, lease a farm and implement a sound deer-management plan. In a few short years, you'll be shooting some great bucks like this one.

INDEX

aerial photos 39
Alberta 204
barriers 81
bedding area 179
beds 36
Ben Brogle 162
big deer individuality 19
BioLogic 213, 216
bleat 77
Brad Farris 108
broadhead 109
buck hole 133
buck reflexes 17
buck senses 15
Bushnell 194
Cabela's 151
call shy 81
Canada 197
climbing stand 85
community scrape 118
convection currents 59
core area 10, 20, 171
cover 45
cover scrape 115
Dakota subspecies 10
Dan Perez 81
David Hale 66, 134

decoy 66, 194

deer management 208

does 48

Don Bell 67

Don Kisky 167

droppings 36

drought 52

dusk flows 58

early season 95

Eliot Strommen 148, 167

Federal 176

fixed-position stand 84

flehmening 70

food 43

food plot 210

food strips 209

full-body harness 92

full moon 172

funnel 24, 80, 122, 134

Gary Roberson 51

gel lures 69

Gore's WindStopper fabric 151

Grant Kuypers 206

Grant Woods, Dr. 210, 212, 215

grunt calling 76

grunt-snort-wheeze 78

Harold Knight 81

Harris bipod 193

home ranges 10, 20

Jim Crumley 209
Jimmy Riley 166
Karl Miller, Dr. 79
Knight & Hale EZ Grunter Plus 82, 194
Knight Magnum DISC 129
ladder stand 86
laser range finder 194
late rut 142
late season 141
Leica 190, 193, 194
Leupold Vari-X Scope 129, 193
Leupold Wind River spotting scope 193
Manitoba 204
Mark Drury 50, 79, 97
Milo Hanson 202
mineral lick 216
mini scrape line 117
Ministikwan 201
mock scrape 68
mock rub 69
moon 49
Mossy Oak 59, 82, 151
Mossy Oak's *Hunting the Country* 169
NRA's *American Hunter* 201
Nikon 194
Nosler Ballistic Tip 176
Nosler Partition 176
nudging 148
observatory stand 91

pheromones 70
post-season scouting 151
pressure 38, 130
Primos' Fightin' Horns 82
Primos' Magnum call 194
public land 135
pushes 163
QDM cooperative 214
Quality Deer Management Association
  (QDMA) 11, 214
range finder 194, 195
rattling 73
Remington 176
rub 35
rub cluster 114
rub line 108, 177
rub urination 71
rut 113
rutting buck body language 127
salivary scent 71
sanctuary 137
Saskatchewan 197, 202, 204
satellite thicket 124
ScentBlocker Plus 59
scent tricks 62
scouting 25
scrapes 35
sheds 151
shooting lane 110
signpost 66

small farm 159
soil test 212
staging area 105
Stony Point shooting sticks 193
Swarovski 190
Terry Drury 79, 100, 168
thermal(s) 56
tier thicket 132
timber block 157
Thompson-Center Encore 209x50 Magnum 129
tracks 35
trail 36
trail camera 41
trail rub 115
trail scrape 115
tree stand 84
tree steps 90
Trophy Bonded Bear Claw 176, 207
Troy Ruiz 101, 169
water 120
weather 46
Weather Channel 48
western whitetails 188
whites 207
Will Primos 51, 78
Winchester 176
wind 53
woodlot 153
Zeiss 190

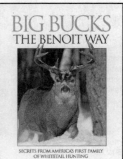